Empress Alexandra

Memories of the Imperial Russian Court

By Maurice Paléologue

Translated by T.C. O'Halloran

ISBN-10:   1731062257
ISBN-13:   978-1731062253

"Empress Alexandra: Memories of the Imperial Russian Court" is the first translation into English of Maurice Paléologue's "Alexandra-Féodorovna: Impératrice de Russie," published in French by Plon in in 1932.

Chapter 1

Describing Marie-Antoinette one day, Chateaubriand said, "Queens have been seen to cry like ordinary women, and it is astonishing how many tears their eyes can hold." By all rights, this epigraph should also be applied to the life of Empress Alexandra, the last Empress of Russia.

Empress Alexandra was born in Darmstadt, on June 6, 1872, to Grand Duke Louis IV of Hesse-Darmstadt and Grand Duchess Alice, daughter of Queen Victoria.

Through the ruling family of Hesse-Darmstadt she could claim the Landgraves of Thuringe and the Dukes of Brabant and Lorraine, as well as St. Elisabeth of Hungary and Mary Stuart.

Having lost her mother at the age of six, she was brought up by her grandmother, Queen Victoria, who took her everywhere with her – to London, to Balmoral, to Windsor, to Sandringham, and to Osborne House on the Isle of Wight. Her education, her training, and the development of her intellect and morality were therefore entirely English, and even at the time I knew her, she was English to the core – in her appearance, in her demeanor, in her rigid and puritanical attitude, in her austere and militant conscience, and indeed in many of her private habits.

In 1894, she became engaged to Nicholas, the Tsarevich of Russia, son of Tsar Alexander III, and this was not an engagement driven by considerations of politics and cold reason, as is so often the case in ruling families. This was an engagement born of love and gentleness, one of the most tender, most romantic, and most high-minded love stories that could ever unite the hearts of ones so young and pure.

The next stage of this story was staged sometimes at the English court, sometimes in the court of the Grand Duke of Hesse-Darmstadt, and sometimes at the Danish court, but wherever they were at the time, it promised Alexandra the guarantee of the brightest of futures from the very beginning. Her fate would assure her the life of a glorious autocrat and she was giddy with the chivalry, the high morality and the profound piety she had discovered in her fiancé's soul.

The mystical and sentimental tone of their engagement is revealed in notes from Alexandra about Nicholas to be found in the Tsarevich's private diaries:

> *Faithful, always waiting on him, always loving him, and always holding out my arms to him ...*

> *Sleep peacefully, and may sweet waves rock you in your cradle! Receive the most tender of kisses from your guardian angel who watches over you ...*

> *Even when we are separated, our hearts are as one. I am always by your side, praying for you, my love ...*

The hour is sounding from the belfry and records each hour, but let us not worry about time as it passes, because, even as it does so, the love between us remains behind. I feel your kisses on my fevered brow. If we ever have to be apart, oh why would it have to be now? Are we not living in a dream from which an awakening would be keen suffering? Oh, do not wake me! Leave me to dream on!

We have captured love and given it wings! It cannot run away, nor can it fly off. It can only sing in our hearts forever ...

I am yours as you are mine. I have locked you in my heart and lost the sweet little key, therefore you will remain locked in there forever ...

I dreamed that I was loved, then I woke up and realized that this was indeed true and thanked God for this on my knees. Real love is a gift from God, a gift that grows and deepens, that becomes stronger and purer by the day ...

There is a true wonder in the love of two beings who are united perfectly together and who hide nothing from each other. They share their joys and sufferings, their happiness and their misfortunes, and from their very first kiss until their deaths they will speak only of love to each other ...

It was not long before Alexandra witnessed her hero being put to the test, because, on November 1, 1894, his father Alexander III died after a short illness at the age of forty-nine.

The Tsarevich adored his father and he was knocked sideways by the Tsar's death, coming as it did while he was still in the prime of his life. However, his sadness was initially for the loss of his father as a man and without consideration for the redoubtable burden that was being placed on his own shoulders.

In his diary, he wrote, 'Death has just called to himself my dear papa whom I loved so much ... Oh what terrible agony! It is the death of a saint ... My head is spinning and I am overcome with grief ... Oh Lord, oh Lord, help me!'

The next day, November 2, he did indeed receive his first indirect help from on high when Alexandra decided to solemnly reject the error of her past Lutheran faith by undertaking to adopt the ancient teachings of the Orthodox Church, inscribing herself among the faithful under the name of Alexandra Feodorovna, clearing the way to their marriage which was then set for twenty-five days' time on November 27.

Unfortunately, the new Autocrat of all the Russias was immediately horrified by the unlimited powers he had inherited; crushed by the legacy his ancestors had handed down to him – the superhuman task of ruling one hundred and fifty million people on the strength of his will and wisdom alone; and at this absolute affirmation of his unchallengeable omnipotence and of his mystical and transcendent powers.

Fortunately, during this painful time, he was courageously supported by his fiancée, Alexandra Feodorovna, who would say to him with the fervor of all the love in her heart, "Have confidence in yourself, my love! God will give you the strength to carry your heavy burden, as it is He who has placed it on your shoulders … Whatever comes our way, suffer it, endure it, and persevere. Don't count how much work you must put in and don't fear any danger! When you suffer the slings and arrows high upon your heavy cross, raise your eyes to God! He will immediately comfort you, my love. The farther and wider he leads you, the more luminous will be our journey …"

Chapter 2

On November 27, 1894, the official mourning of the court was lifted for the celebration of the imperial marriage. The ceremony took place in the church of the Winter Palace, the huge and grandiose palace on the banks of the Neva that epitomizes all the glories of the Romanovs. The sanctuary, with its fabulous wealth, and Asiatic and Byzantine sense of luxury, shone with supernatural light in an embarrassment of rubies, sapphires, topazes and emeralds.

Alexandra Feodorovna was wearing the ancient costume of the Muscovite empresses, a white silk dress emblazoned with silver, a court gown brocaded with gold, trailing a train that was so long and heavy that it took no less than five chamberlains to ease it along its way. The weight of the magnificent accoutrements emphasized her willowy shape, and the dazzling and bejeweled diadem that crowned her head illuminated the faultlessness of her face, the exactness of her features, and the solemn and willing expression in her eyes.

Two days after this great day, Nicholas wrote in his diary, 'Blessings to you, oh Lord, for the ineffable happiness you have laid upon me because it surpasses anything I could have dreamed of.' Alexandra wrote next to it, 'I could never have imagined that there could ever be in this world such good fortune, such a fusion between two people … I love you! I love you! These words sum up everything in my life so far.'

The young sovereigns therefore set out on their conjugal path with every blessing. To quote the beautiful image conjured up by Milton, they "embraced each other in Paradise."

But when she emerged from her paradisiac haze, the new Tsarina found herself breathing in quite a different atmosphere. She soon realized that the court and the public were more inclined to extend to her respect rather than sympathy, and even an incomprehensible coldness, because during the course of the formal marriage ceremony, of the moving liturgy enshrined within the Winter Palace, many could not keep from crying. Emperor Alexander III, the late "Emperor Saint," was mourned by all, and by the people at large as much as by his own family.

Amid this intensely sad setting, many judged their new Empress most unfavorably. With a rigid pretentiousness and from a lofty dryness they looked down on her all-too-visible efforts to control the emotions that threatened to overwhelm her, her ineffable emotions of light and love. They did not even hold back from opining, "Oh how our excellent Dowager-Empress, our beloved Marie Feodorovna, is so much more gracious than her! Remember how she conquered our hearts from the very first time we ever set eyes on her!"

The criticism was even unkinder among the ordinary people. "Celebrating a marriage so soon after a funeral does not bode well." Worse, in lowered, frightened voices, they whispered, "*Nemka!* The German woman with the evil eye."

During the following months, this cruel impression continued to feed gossip around the court, as well as infiltrating itself and rooting itself among the masses.

One dramatic incident immediately entrenched their prejudices once and for all.

During the sacred solemnities of the coronation in Moscow, the precautions taken by the police on the great expanse of the Khodinsky Field, where the popular celebrations were taking place, were so badly planned that two thousand peasants ('*moujiks*') were crushed to death amid the horrendous confusion.

That evening, the Sovereigns had agreed to attend a great ball put on by the Count of Montebello, the French Ambassador. The traditions of the imperial court were so set in stone that it was inconceivable that such an event should be cancelled, therefore the Tsar and Tsarina attended the ball. However, throughout the evening, the Moscow crowds pressed themselves up against the glittering windows of the palace, muttering, "The *Nemka* is dancing! Why would she care that thousands of us died this morning? No wonder she takes funerals in her stride!"

This disastrous sequence of events continued; several weeks later, the Sovereigns visited Kiev, the second most sacred city of Russia, the ancient and venerated capital of St. Vladimir, and there, right in front of their eyes, a boat carrying three hundred spectators slipped below the waters of the River Dnieper.

And inauspicious incidents continued to build up around the imperial couple as, day after day, superstitions grew and grew. "Because of the nefarious influence of the *Nemka*, our Emperor is headed for catastrophe."

Chapter 3

But of all the resentments that the Russian people held against the poor Empress, there was one that afflicted her in particular because it related to the most sensitive, the deepest, the most intimate aspects of her physical and moral being.

What is the first duty of a queen, her greatest responsibility, almost her most critical function on behalf of the state? It is to ensure the future of the dynasty by producing male heirs.

A year after their marriage, Alexandra Feodorovna produced a daughter; two years later, she produced a second daughter; two years after that, she produced a third daughter. It was in vain that she prayed to God to give her a son; it was in vain that she increased the frequency of her prayers, her penitence, her fasts, her pilgrimages, and all the disciplines and abject pieties of her Russian faith.

On June 18, 1901, she produced a fourth child, an event that the superstitious masses did not fail to mark by their habitual refrain, "As we have always said, the *Nemka*, the German woman, has the evil eye. Because of her nefarious influence, our Emperor is headed for catastrophe."

In her desperation, Alexandra Feodorovna decided to have recourse to some strange and bizarre artifices. This is why, in the month of September 1901, while accompanying the Tsar in France, she made the acquaintance of a fantastical person, a magician from Lyon, Philippe Nizier, who

15

had been recommended to her by Grand Duchess Militza, the wife of Grand Duke Peter, and by her sister, Princess Anastasia, Duchess of Leuchtenberg, the future wife of Grand Duke Nicholas.

Born in 1849, and the son of poor agricultural workers, the young Philippe was looked after from a young age by his uncles who ran a modest butcher's shop in Lyon in the quarter known as the Croix-Rousse. From his fifteenth birthday, the boy started manifesting some strange characteristics ranging from a preference for being alone, a fascination with the mysteries, a lively interest in sorcery, and a taste for the Tarot, hypnotizers and sleepwalkers. Soon he was working hard to gain skills in occult medicine, and from the beginning he succeeded.

In 1872, after leaving his uncles' butcher's shop, he opened an office at 4 Boulevard du Nord, where he treated his patients with psychic fluids and astral forces. Rather overweight and of average height, simple in his manner, sober in his behavior, with a quiet voice, a high forehead under coarse brown hair, and a gently attractive and penetrating expression, he proved easily capable of establishing great sympathy and empathy over all those who came to him for help.

In September 1877, he married one of his patients, Jeanne Landar, whom he had cured and with whom he would soon have a girl.

In 1887, he was denounced by the doctors of Lyon for practicing medicine without a license and was given a fine. However, as is often the case, this punishment only served to make him even more fashionable. In 1890 and 1892 he again appeared before a judge, who fined him again, although all three court cases worked out to his benefit. All the witnesses, even the ones where he had failed to effect a cure, were of one accord in praising his caring nature, his sense of pity, his dispassionate concern, his consoling and comforting attentions, and the relaxing gentleness that exuded from each and every one of his mannerisms.

In order to bring himself into compliance with the law, Philippe decided in future that he would associate himself with a Polish homeopath, Steintzy, who had gained a valid diploma and who countersigned his prescriptions.

His office, now at 35 Rue de la Tête-d'Or, was as busy as ever, and artisans, shop workers, concierges, and chefs still made up the bulk of his clientele. However, from 1896, they were joined by people of Society, ladies of standing, judges, actresses, officers and priests. The tobacconist who ran the shop opposite his office, and who kept the police informed of his activities, confessed herself "stunned by the fashionable people who visit him."

One day, two Russian ladies, Madames S..... and P....., who were undergoing surgery in a clinic in Lyon, decided that they could no longer resist the temptation of being treated by this healer, and the butcher's boy astonished them with his clairvoyance, with his supernatural powers, and with the towering simplicity of his therapeutic treatments, whereupon they persuaded him to follow them to Cannes where they introduced him to their friends, the Grand Duchesses Militza and Anastasia.

Under the protection of such high patronage, Philippe presented himself on September 20, 1901, at the Compiègne Palace, where the Under-Superintendent of the Russian Police in France was responsible for examining him prior to his being introduced to the Sovereigns. Extremely distrustful by nature and very skilled in his arts, this agent of the Okhrana found himself fully reassured by the simple and reserved behavior of this large man with his voluminous mustache who could have been mistaken for a Sunday school teacher. From his appearance, there was only one thing that intrigued him – a little triangle of black silk that he carried around his neck which he claimed to be an extremely precious talisman that he would never be separated from.

From the very first meeting, Philippe seduced the Sovereigns, who decided on the spot to invite him to Russia. He left France almost immediately and a house was prepared for him at Tsarskoe Selo.

From there he gained the complete confidence of his imperial hosts, who, apart from his magical talents, appreciated greatly his tranquil air and his utter discretion. Once or twice a week he would meet them to conduct sessions involving hypnosis, prophecies, incantations and necromancy, and the pliable will of the Emperor took strength from these nocturnal exercises during which several of his resolutions were dictated according to the wishes of the shade of Alexander III. And, as far as matters of health went, Philippe's advice was considered authoritative.

But during the confidences exchanged between the Sovereigns and Philippe, there was one subject that was reserved for them alone, a truly intimate secret, a State secret that was at the same time a secret to be guarded in the utmost privacy.

The Emperor, the Empress and the Russian people were all awaiting anxiously the birth of a male heir – the Tsarevich – and as Philip claimed that all the arcane powers of nature were at his fingertips, he pretended that he could not only identify the sex of a child in the womb, but that he could even change the sex of the child. By combining his skills in transcendental medicine, astromancy and psycho-surgery, the healer could bring under his control embryonic development, however complicated that might be to achieve!

In the spring of 1902, Alexandra Feodorovna became pregnant again, and this time she was in no doubt that she was carrying a son. The Emperor was equally convinced, and Philippe encouraged their belief.

But on September 1, the Empress felt a sudden pain, and before anyone could come to help her, she saw all her hopes dashed.

This trick of fate dealt a cruel blow to Philippe's prestige as it was claimed that the Empress had never really been pregnant at all, and that her apparent physical state had not been real but rather entirely caused by her psychological one. When the truth of the situation soon emerged, the facts served as a mark against the healer from Lyon within the court, but the Emperor and Empress maintained their confidence in him, listened tolerantly to his explanations, and remained convinced of his magical powers. Nevertheless they were sensitive to the secret advice proffered to them from religious circles, and the Empress' confessor, Bishop Feofan, for whom they held great affection, succeeded in throwing their souls into a troubled state. Hadn't their belief in the occult lured them beyond the bounds of the permissible? Hadn't their deception about the nature of things been a warning from God?

This time the Sovereigns did not dare to resist and so they abandoned the healer, who returned to France with great sadness.

After the grandeur and luxury of Tsarskoe Selo, the Tête-d'Or Quarter offered only the desolation of the commonplace, and in returning to his banal office and renewing contact with his undistinguished former clientele, he encountered all the bitterness that comes from human disgrace.

Subjected to many and varied sorrows, he found that he could no longer ply his trade and he soon retreated to the countryside around the Arbresle, where he died of tuberculosis on August 2, 1906.

After the magician was removed from their lives, the Sovereigns realized the extreme gravity of their all-too-long aberration and felt the need to make a great display of their respect for the Orthodox faith, whereupon, after a pious lack of interest and considerable procrastination, the Sacred Synod recommended an investigation into the canonization of an obscure monk, the Blessed Seraphim, who around 1820 had died "in the odor of sanctity" at the monastery of Sarov, near Tambov.

This affair, which was of no interest to anyone, led to an enquiry that dragged on forever and that was subjected to the oblivion of endless adjournments. Also, those proposing the canonization found themselves confronted with a serious objection: the body of this ascetic man had passed through all the usual stages of decomposition, while the Orthodox Church insisted that the incorruptibility of the human form after death was a precondition for sainthood.

Whatever their reasons, the Tsar and Tsarina then decided to take a passionate interest in the glorification of this blessed soul, and, in his role as Supreme Head of the Church, Nicholas II demanded to be kept informed, in the minutest detail, concerning every aspect of the proceedings and that a conclusion should be reached as quickly as possible.

This became a new obsession for the Sovereigns and they were continuously to be found in audience with the Metropolitans of St. Petersburg, Kiev, and Moscow; with the Procurator for the Sacred Synod; with the Bishop of Tambov; and with the Archimandrite of Sarov. And what particularly pleased them was that their dearly beloved Philippe, whose magic encompassed a large amount of naïve piety, supported them from afar in their zeal.

It didn't take much to wake up the Sacred Synod, which quickly discovered in the ascetic Seraphim a great accumulation of undoubted virtues, qualities and prodigies, and then, as if by magic, all difficulties were overcome, all delays were foreshortened, and the process passed beyond the realm of any further objections.

On January 14, 1903, the Metropolitan of Moscow submitted a report to the Emperor concluding:

1. That the Blessed Seraphim should be added to the list of saints;

2. That his remains should be put on display as holy relics;

3. That a service should be established in his honor.

The Tsar wrote on the bottom of the report, "Read with a feeling of indescribable joy and profound affection."

The decree of canonization, sealed with imperial approval, was published on February 11, 1903, and it only remained for it to be celebrated with the papal liturgies that definitively raise a blessed man to the ranks of the saints.

The Emperor decided that this celebration should be surrounded with the utmost ceremony and even took part in the rites in person, accompanied by the Empress and the entire imperial family.

The preparations took several months but the canonization rites were finally started on July 30. For a whole week, all the top-ranking clergy of the Empire arrived in Sarov, along with thousands of priests, monks and nuns, a whole crowd of bureaucrats and government officers, and finally a diverse and confused mass of one hundred thousand pilgrims.

The Sovereigns arrived in the evening and were greeted with the chanting of hymns and the ringing of bells. A hurricane of acclamations followed them on their progress. The Office for the Dead filled the night air right through to the dawn.

The next day, July 31, began with a morning Eucharistic Mass, with the Sovereigns approaching the altar. In the afternoon, a funeral service took place for the repose of the soul that was to be set in glory. During the evening, the body of Seraphim was paraded around the churches and the monastery, with the Emperor as one of the pallbearers. Around midnight, the precious relics were uncovered and exposed for the first time for the veneration by the faithful. After that, orisons, litanies and psalms followed one after the other without a moment's pause, until the next morning.

On August 1, Bishop Anthony, the Metropolitan of St. Petersburg, celebrated a grand papal Mass, lasting nearly four hours, for the canonization itself. As evening approached, Seraphim's coffin was once again carried in procession across the town and around the monastery. Predications, panegyrics, cries of Hallelujah, and a whole series of minor offices followed throughout the next day.

Finally, on August 3, to bring these innumerable liturgies to an end, a newly-built church was consecrated in the name of the new saint.

Chapter 4

Returning with their spirits all aglow from the prodigious and prestigious splendors of Sarov, the Emperor immediately had to deal with a serious dispute that had been building up over several months between Russia and Japan over the status of Korea.

In both countries national sentiments had flared and were intensifying with each day that passed. Peace initiatives, hosted by the French government, collapsed one after the other. Filled with mystical dreams, and egged on by his cousin Kaiser Wilhelm II, the Tsar became convinced that Fate had bestowed upon him the sacred mission of spreading Christianity along the entire coast of the Pacific Ocean. For several months, his "dear Willy" had ceaselessly intoned to him, "God has visibly handed down to you the destiny of making Christ's law triumphant across the whole of the Far East, therefore you must acquire both Manchuria and Korea."

Nonetheless, the Tsar hesitated for a while, turning the matter over in his mind and switching from one point of view to the next, not realizing that his irresolution and equivocation was making war inevitable.

On February 7, 1904, hostilities began abruptly when the Japanese navy made a night attack on the Russian flank at Port Arthur, and to the surprise of the entire world, it was soon clear that, through ignorance and weakness, Nicholas II had thrown himself into an adventure that could only lead to disaster.

After seven months of mortifying setbacks, continuous retreat, disappointments, failed counter-attacks, feebleness and humiliation, the Russian people began to complain angrily against the Romanovs.

Then, on August 12, a happy event suddenly reignited national enthusiasm: the Empress gave birth to a son. At last the Emperor had an heir! Russia had its Tsarevich!

From then on, Alexandra Feodorovna entered a new life. It had been nearly ten years since she had become Empress and she had never interested herself in politics. Certainly, the couple who never left each other's side and who lived a life of calm and intimate retreat, gossiped among themselves about matters of state, but the Empress only had one opinion on every issue and in every circumstance – that of her husband.

However, toward the end of 1904, the long line of Russian army defeats in Manchuria abruptly and terrifyingly awoke passionate revolutionary feelings across the length and breadth of the Empire. In 1905, the disastrous battles of Mukden and Tsushima drove public indignation to fever pitch, and a new and serious event marked each day. Riots, lootings, fires, attempted assassinations and plotting never ceased, and, more often than not, it proved impossible to suppress these outbreaks because the army refused to get involved.

By the autumn of 1906, despite the signing of a peace treaty with Japan, the civil disorders had become so widespread and so violent that the whole structure of tsarism seemed to be on the brink of collapse. Nicholas II, therefore, finally realized that he needed to give way and accept the establishment of a representative parliament, a 'Duma,' to help rule his empire, although he ensured that its powers were so severely limited that, in truth, it could only act as an advisory assembly. Nevertheless, it was the first time that an imperial Autocrat had ever condescended to discuss the affairs of state with nationally elected representatives.

It was not surprising, then, that the Tsar hesitated for a long time before agreeing to this because it caused him such extreme anxiety to choose to resign himself to a reduction in his supreme authority which his conscience led him to believe made him directly answerable to God Himself. But, in this period of inner turmoil, what made him the saddest of all was that the Empress argued against this move.

"No," she said heatedly, "you do not have a single right to hand over even the tiniest part of your authority to your subjects because Fate itself conferred it upon you ... You have no more right to renounce the Autocracy than to renounce your Orthodox faith. God Himself gave you this power as a sacred duty and it is to God Himself that you will have to account for your actions one day ... When all is said and done, you are merely a trustee of your power. Your ancestors passed it on to you in its entirety and you must do the same one day for your son."

In saying this, she was expressing a great historical truth, a great axiom of state and divine law. In the eyes of the Russian people, the majesty of the Tsar was in its essence mystical. The Church consecrated and sanctified imperial power to the extent that the Autocracy and the Orthodoxy seemed two halves of one august and indivisible essence. The spiritual and the temporal were so intertwined that religious and social affairs could not be imagined the one without the other.

Yet, in the face of the brutal pressure of events, Nicholas II gave way before public demands, and on May 10, 1906, amid the imposing surroundings of the Winter Palace, he solemnly opened the new parliament (Duma).

However, his address to the members of this parliament revealed only too clearly his private reservations about what he was being forced to do.

"Concern for the greater interest with which I have been charged by Divine Providence has decided that I should convoke an assembly of representatives of my people to collaborate with me in the preparation of laws, because my deepest wish is to see Russia happy and to leave a solid inheritance to my son. I therefore salute you, men of competence, whom I have ordered my dear subjects to elect. Get to work immediately and show yourselves worthy of my faith in you. And may God help you in this task."

This recitation produced among every one of his audience, whatever their political leanings, the most disastrous of effects. With his pallid face, his trembling hands, and a voice sounding almost as if it was being strangled in his throat, Nicholas II stuttered his way through his sentences in this piteous harangue, which he had conceived as being lofty and feisty, rather than pronouncing them clearly. Toward the end, in fact, everyone thought he was going to faint, so anguished was his appearance, so stressed, so skeletal.

Nevertheless, order did begin to reestablish itself across that colossal territory. The revolutionary strikes, the mutinies within the navy and the army, and the massacres of the Jews became rarer and were suppressed more easily. Only the most fanatical of the terrorists continued on their course and hardly a week went by without some high functionary – a provincial governor, a military police officer, a prison governor, a chief of police – falling victim to the bullets or the bombs of an anarchist.

And through a sort of collective psychosis or a bizarre mental contagion, these constantly recurring crimes inflamed the populace more than it frightened them, because they secretly admired the unheard of audacity of the outrages, the shadowy plotting of the conspirators, and, above all, the astonishing bravura of the assassins, their contempt in the face of death, their insolence in front of the judges, and their fortitude on the scaffold itself.

It would be three long years before Russia recovered its stability inside its borders and its prestige abroad.

Chapter 5

These three years were critical in the life of Alexandra Feodorovna.

When the Tsar addressed the Duma, expressing his wish to "leave my son a solid inheritance," he was reflecting the constant worry of his Empress because, for all of the spectacle laid out before her, her everyday life laid bare how this glorious heritage was in reality as threatened and as precarious as it could possibly be.

At the same time, the plots being fomented against the Emperor bore witness to the courage and determination that was required to maintain a massive surveillance operation around him, protecting him by means of an impenetrable barrier of police, military police and Cossacks. Day and night he had to be guarded, even within his private apartments, even under the windows and in front of the doors of his bedroom, giving the Empress a constant sense of what destiny was holding in store for her husband and her children.

But another concern, far more disturbing, would soon test her nerves, which were already stretched to the full, still further.

Alexandra Feodorovna's son, whom she adored obsessively, began to show signs over several months of a strange illness that troubled the doctors because none of them dared to formulate a precise diagnosis of his affliction.

With the insight of her maternal instincts, Alexandra Feodorovna was the first to see things truly as they were, only too aware as she was of the medical inheritance of her family, examples of which lay all too close to home. She was in no doubt: the specific symptoms they were observing in the child belonged to that strange and incurable illness, hemophilia. One of her uncles, the Duke of Albany – a son of Queen Victoria – had died of it. She also had personally watched one of her young brothers – Frederick William of Hesse – and two young sons of her sister, Princess Irene – wife of Prince Henry of Prussia – die in the same way.

However, the doctors continued to assure her that they had yet to see all the symptoms characteristic of hemophilia. Besides, modern science had come up with several new ways of renewing a patient's blood. In short, there was still plenty of room for both doubt and hope.

But these attempted assurances failed to dispel her profound anxiety about her son's illness, and she continually suffered the shame and remorse associated with the suspicion that, through her selfishness, she was physiologically responsible for the terrible illness that had befallen her son.

From this day, and over the next few months, she began to develop symptoms of severe physical and mental distress: insomnia, difficulty in breathing, heart trouble, migraines, alternating sensations of heat and cold, vertigo, pins and needles, trembling, palpitations, faintness, anxiety, a permanent imbalance in her senses, and all the capricious and disconcerting examples of emotional and psychological neurosis as her character and physical disposition changed accordingly.

She was just thirty-five years old and still beautiful, tall and slim. Now her face became hard, and at times would suddenly grow either pale or blotchy. Her eyes occasionally took on a strange intensity, somber and fixed; or for several hours her expression would become dim and appear sad as her mouth and eyebrows contracted. An overwhelming exhaustion, without apparent cause, often disabled her and all interaction with the world would then prove beyond her. The anticipation of all future ceremonial duties terrified her because she feared that her strength would abandon her.

Therefore, she confined herself more and more to the narrow circle of her immediate family. She avoided St. Petersburg and only wanted to live at Tsarskoe Selo, Peterhof, or, better still, Livadia on the distant shoreline of the Crimea. The Emperor never tried to contradict her wishes, not only out of pity, but also because his own simple tastes and natural shyness attracted him equally to the life of a recluse.

In the past no court in Europe could match the Romanov court for the extravagance of its spectacles, for the wealth of its costumes and liveries, for the magnificence of its processions and parades, for the smartness of its uniforms and grooming, for the brilliance of its ornamentation and jewelry, and for the extraordinary impression of stability and power that pervaded all its ceremonies.

Between the autumn months and the summer, with a break only for Holy Week, there was a long series of balls, concerts, and suppers, not to mention all the court receptions, at the Winter Palace. The grand dukes and grand duchesses, the diplomatic corps, the dignitaries and the generals, the ministers and passing foreigners were continuously invited to share a table with the Tsar. In their turn, the Sovereigns would also accept invitations to dine with ambassadors and members of the old Russian aristocracy: the Orlovs, the Bariatinskys, the Tcheremetievs, the Dolgorukys, the Schuvalovs, the Troubetskoys, the Belosselskys and the Vorontsovs.

Now all this was over. The ill-health of Alexandra Feodorovna served as the reason, or the pretext, to cancel one by one all the balls, all the concerts, all the receptions and even the dinners for the family. Soon the Sovereigns were surrounded by a void. The grand dukes and grand duchesses rarely saw them. Other than during unavoidable meetings between Nicholas II and his ministers and a few bureaucrats, no voice, no breath of fresh air from the outside world any longer penetrated the silent and cloistered atmosphere of the imperial palaces.

From now on, with no calls on her time, hidden away from the world, and reduced to the society only of her husband and her children, Alexandra Feodorovna devoted long hours every day to dark thoughts, to reading and meditating upon religious matters, and the to the uplifting dreams and practices of Orthodox mysticism.

To frame her devotions in a more intimate manner, she ordered the construction of the Feodorovsky Sobor – a little church designed according to the old Muscovite style – amid the wooded surroundings of their palace at Tsarskoe Selo. She herself laid down how it should be built and decorated, with a desire that it should be glorious in its splendor but containing underground oratories, low ceilinged crypts and hidden alcoves, where shadows would float, the candles would glimmer, and the fumes of the incense, and the shimmering of the light off the gold and the stone, would fill the soul with sublime ecstasy.

She therefore drew together the most beautiful works of art Russian piety could imagine for the celebration of its liturgies, a dazzling treasure of crosses, icons, decorated gospels and missals, triptychs, chalices, ciboria, chasubles, enamels, rugs and precious fabrics so that the whole church would shine with a sumptuous and supernatural life like a tabernacle.

Dotted about under the high wooden carving that surrounds the sanctuary there are simple houses with galleries and towers painted in lively colors depicting the picturesque architecture of the ancient town of Novgorod, the barracks lodging those most devoted guardians of the throne – the faithful Cossacks of the Escort, and this ancient military enclosure, with its medieval aspect and its reference to a past age, emphasizes all the more the fierce isolation of the Feodrovsky Sobor.

The archaic and passionate mysticism of the Empress would quickly become ever more developed as her emotional breakdown intensified.

In considering signs of the Empress' mental state, a curious spiritual conundrum arises: How is it that a foreign princess, a German by birth, a Lutheran by baptism, an English woman by education – this pure-blooded Westerner – was suffused so quickly, so radically, so persuasively and captivatingly, by all the aspects of Russian mysticism in its most Eastern, archaic and alien form? This, it might appear, presents us with a psychological paradox.

The solution is simple: it was already established in her from the start because of her heredity. All this neurosis, all this hyper-emotionality, all this hysteria, lethargy and irritability, all this propensity toward mystical ecstasy had been handed down to her across many generations.

Grand Duchess Elisabeth, the Empress' older sister, had a similarly strange ardor in her religious beliefs. After the assassination in 1905 of her husband, Grand Duke Sergei, the Governor of Moscow, she founded a women's religious community under the title of "Martha and Mary," appointing herself its Abbess, which she ran with an inflamed zeal. Most pure in her heart and in her thoughts, until then she had dazzled the world with her beauty, but now she restricted herself to following the most rigorous practices of asceticism, penitence and charity, in continual mediation of the Calvary, in an insatiable desire to break herself, to drown herself, to annihilate herself in front of God.

This same predisposition to religious fervor, this same compulsive attraction to mysticism, albeit to a lesser extent, could be found in their mother, Princess Alice, the daughter of Queen Victoria who married the heir to the Grand Duchy of Hesse-Darmstadt in 1862. Raised according to the precepts of High Anglicanism, she conceived, from the time of her arrival in Darmstadt, a strange spiritual and intellectual passion for David Strauss, the great rationalist theologian of Tubingue and the famous author of 'The Life of Jesus.' Under the guise of Swabian Philistinism, this defrocked priest was the most Romanesque of men. He had known all the sorcery of the "eternally feminine," and all the temptations and disappointments of love. In time, a great fatigue overcame him. Disgusted by the essence of his labors, and even more so by himself, tired of a life from which he no longer expected anything, he became a nihilist and aspired to the Great Nothing. This is when he met Princess Alice.

There is a profound mystery around the interaction of their intellects and their souls, however there is no doubt that David Strauss deeply troubled her beliefs and that she suffered terrible crises.

Under the weight of such a legacy, Alexandra Feodorovna was fated to an excessive religious sensitivity. It is quite possible that, even if she had continued to live at the English court, she would equally have succumbed to a dangerous attraction to mystical spiritualism, to the examples of the "enlightened" that you find among certain evangelical brotherhoods. But there her mysticism would have been constrained and tempered by the generally strong and healthy public attitude toward spiritual matters as channeled through official theology, by the sober coldness and monotony of the rites, by reflection and positivity, and by the practical piety of the Anglo-Saxon race.

However, as it turned out, her destiny was to live the rest of her life in a land where, over the centuries, mysticism had dominated the souls of all, where the long-held, inalterable cult of the Byzantine had cloaked all the most moving and esthetic modes.

Her destiny had decided further that, as the Empress of Russia, she would have to take part constantly in the splendid ceremonies of the Orthodox faith, each time to be shaken by them to the center of her being.

The majestic nature of the role she played on the world stage obliged her to live her life amid that which would inevitably exacerbate her hereditary nervous condition.

Chapter 6

This life of hers, cut off from the world as she was, and absorbed in her devotions, fatally exposed the Empress to the direct influence, without the benefit of restraining forces, of the few people who could still get close to her.

This is how a simple maid of honor who served her as a modest secretary, Miss Anna Alexandrovna Tanayev, in time exerted a powerful influence over her.

Anna belonged to an old Russian family of the lesser nobility who, since the reign of Alexander I, had offered unbroken service to the imperial family as court bureaucrats. Her father, Alexander Sergeievich Taneyev, was Head of the Private Chancellery of the Tsar. Her mother was born a Tolstoy and could proudly count among her ancestors the 1812 savior of the Russia people, Marshall Kutusov.

Thirty-three years of age, with a round head, high coloring, bright eyes, fleshy lips, an ample shape, and completely provincial in her dress and her grooming, the Empress' new secretary took up her service at Tsarskoe Selo in February 1905 in the midst of a great tragedy. The court had only just learned of the assassination of Grand Duke Sergei, the Governor-General of Moscow, an uncle of the Emperor and a brother-in-law of the Empress. And of all the violent acts that the revolutionaries had gloried in over the previous few months, this was by far the most horrible and the most audacious.

At three o'clock in the afternoon, as the Grand Duke was crossing the Kremlin in his car, a terrorist threw a bomb at him, hitting him in the chest and blowing him to pieces. His wife, the Grand Duchess Elisabeth, was also in the Kremlin where she was organizing work for the Red Cross to help the Russian armies in Manchuria. Hearing the horrendous explosion, she ran out into the courtyard as fast as she could, without even putting on her hat, and started to collect together with her beautiful hands the head, the arms, the legs and all the remains of her husband that had been blasted across the snow, now soaked in blood.

This shock violently affected the Empress' nerves because she saw in this not only a political assassination and the murder of a haughty and pitiless grand duke who was regarded across the whole of Russia as the leading figure in the current reactionary crusade against the revolutionaries. She also saw it, above all, as a monstrous sacrilege, because the plotters had decided to stage their endeavor in the Moscow Kremlin, the most venerated of the country's sanctuaries, the place where the Romanovs had first received their fateful mission of establishing a kingdom on Russian soil.

The Empress had spent much of her time in her prayers, penitences and mortifications during the Lent that started soon after this outrage, but she believed she saw in her young secretary a shy level of generosity toward her, and a comprehensive and discreet sense of sympathy for this most heavy testing of her soul.

A tender friendship between them soon followed, and the two women spent many hours a day in each other's company, almost always in the mauve boudoir next to the Empress' bedroom, mostly occupying themselves with reading and music. When not doing this, they would sew interminably together, breaking off to opine on mystical matters or to engage in silent reverie, hand in hand, gazing into each other's eyes, as they sat side-by-side on a large sofa that stretched across the whole of one end of the room.

"Each day," the Empress would tell the young girl, "I thank God for having sent me such a friend as you!"

The inexplicable, captivating and feverish intimacy that developed between them set all of St. Petersburg Society talking.

In May 1907, at the instigation and under the patronage of the Empress, Anna Tanayeva married a naval officer who was a hero of the Russo-Japanese War, Lt. Alexander Vassilievich Vyrubov. The wedding ceremony was celebrated at Tsarskoe Selo, in the great court church, in the presence of the Sovereigns, with such pomp, completely unjustified by the subaltern rank of the husband, that it set off another round of malicious public gossip.

The young couple came to live within two hundred meters of the Alexander Palace, in a little house they had been given by the Empress which had been furnished with a telephone line that connected directly to the imperial apartments.

No one was surprised when, a few months later, it was learned that, without a single explanation, Alexander Vyrubov had obtained a divorce from his wife.

It seems that about the same time the tortured Alexandra Feodorovna suddenly experienced a great secret trouble, a strange and sad story, interrupted mysteriously by a sudden death that rendered the tender and passionate companionship of her young favorite more indispensable than ever.

Chapter 7

During her engagement, Anna Tanayeva happened to meet a bizarre "pilgrim" at the house of Grand Duchess Militza, the wife of Grand Duke Peter. This pilgrim hailed from Siberia and brought with him the fantastical air of a divine healer. His name was Grigory Efimovich Rasputin.

He was a peasant, a simple *moujik*, a man from the lowest rank in society. He was born in 1871 in the village of Pokrovskoe, near Tobolsk. His father, Efim Novy, was a horse trader who had honestly acquired a certain wealth by the secret buying and selling of stolen horses.

The nickname of "Rasputin" that was accorded to the young Grigory by his friends defined that time of his life and foretold what was to come. "Rasputin" is a rural slang term for "the lecher," "the lay-about," or "the scoundrel."

Often beaten away by fathers or whipped publicly by the police, one day Grigory met his road to Damascus. The exhortations of a priest, to whom he was giving a ride by cart to the famous sanctuary of Abalaksk, near Tobolsk, instigated in him a sudden revelation of his powerful and luminous instincts for mysticism. Soon afterward, the Virgin Mary deigned to make a blessed appearance before him, setting him off on the path to salvation, accompanied by inner voices assuring him that, whatever his past abominations, a great task had been reserved for him by Fate.

So, immediately picking up the staff of a pilgrim, he went to the wonderful *Lavra* [a collection of monastic buildings] of

Kiev, then to the *lavra* at Troitsa near Moscow, and then to the Pochayiv *Lavra* near Rovno.

For the next three years he tramped as a vagabond from monastery to monastery, planning to crown his pilgrimage with the worthy goal of reaching the rough and distant sacred monasteries on Mount Athos.

What could have been going through the mind of this Siberian *moujik* the day that he left his house in Pokrovskoe and undertook such a sacred odyssey which would lead him so far and so high? Whatever it was, it was beyond the understanding of all our Western psychology, but that powerful storyteller, that delightful visionary, Dostoyevsky, explains it well enough in this striking image of a Russian peasant.

> *Sometimes, in the middle of a forest, you will encounter a moujik wearing a tattered caftan. He is still; he seems to be thinking, but he is not; he is lost in an obscure dream. If you were to touch him, he would jump and look at you without understanding, like one who is sleeping suddenly coming awake. He would come to very quickly, but if you were to ask him what his dream was about, he wouldn't know because he will have remembered nothing of it. Nonetheless, he will retain from this trance some profound impressions that will please him and that will build up inside his subconscious.*

One day, after maybe a year of such reveries,
he will leave, he will leave everything, and he
will travel to Jerusalem for his salvation, or
maybe he will burn down his village, or maybe
he'll commit a crime first and then start off on
his pilgrimage. There are many such souls
among our people ...

After spending three years as an idle, if devout, vagabond, Rasputin had completely lost his desire to live a sedentary life and to work day-in, day-out, so he began wandering from town to town picking up what easy and short term work he could, begging for alms and somewhere to stay at the gates of every monastery, certain always to obtain a morsel of bread for the asking "in the name of Christ," entertaining himself in his indolence with debauchery and religiosity.

And all the time his mystical instincts grew stronger; the robustness of his temperament, the ardor of his senses, and the unrestrained courage of his imagination, drove him on relentlessly. This is how he came to join that lubricious sect known as the *"Khlysty"* or "flagellants," and how he demonstrated once again the extent to which he was quintessentially Russian in the dynamics of his nature, in his every thought and in his every idea; how his strong and deep roots dug forcefully into the Russian soil.

This point is worthy of greater explanation.

Alongside the official Orthodox faith, which is so imposing and so full of pomp, but so strictly inclined to serve the interests of the Tsar, the people have developed any number of more or less clandestine sects whose bizarre rites express every form and every variation possible of religious belief, from the most idealized to the most ignoble, with an indomitable inclination toward anarchy, outlandishness and absurdity.

First of all there is the austere congregation of the *Raskol*, founded on the premise of establishing a direct communication between the human soul and God, denying that the clergy are credible and indispensable mediators between the Heavenly Father and mankind.

Then there are the *Doukhobors*, who only accept one source of faith – intuition – and who refuse to participate in military service in order to avoid the spilling of blood.

The *Beglopopovtsy* renounce the demonic servitude of the official church.

The *Molokanes*, the "milk drinkers," seek to live the pure Christian life in all its integrity.

The *Stranniky*, the "wanderers," seek to escape the Kingdom of the Antichrist by traveling indefinitely across the steppes and the frozen forests of Siberia.

The *Chtoundistes* preach agrarian communism to bring to an end the reign of the Pharaohs.

The *Khlysty* feel Christ incarnating among them during their erotic ecstasies.

The *Skoptzy* castrate themselves to avoid carnal temptation.

The *Bialoritzy*, who dress themselves entirely in white like heavenly angels, travel from village to village proclaiming the importance of innocence.

The *Pomortsy* renounce the baptism of children before adulthood because the Antichrist rules the church and they must therefore renew their baptismal sacraments of their own free will as adults.

The *Nikoudichniky*, extreme deniers of social order, seek on earth that far-off place of Jesus' real kingdom where sin is impossible.

The *Douchitely*, the "stranglers," throttle the dying out of human pity and in retrospective sympathy for Jesus' own Calvary.

And there are lots more – a hundred more – accounting for as many as twelve million believers in total.

The *Khlisty* sect, which is the sect that Rasputin chose, distinguishes itself by the extravagance and sensuality of its practices. Its adherents, around 120,000 of them, mostly inhabit the regions of Kazan, Simbirsk, Saratov, Oufa, Orenbourg and Tobolsk. The highest spirituality seems to animate their doctrine because they want nothing less than to communicate directly with God, to spread the Word, and to incarnate Christ. However, to attain this celestial communion, they stray into all the follies of the flesh. The faithful, both men and women, get together at night, sometimes in a small house and sometimes in the clearing in a forest. There, while invoking the presence of God, singing hymns and giving voice to canticles, they dance in a circle at an ever more furious pace, while the person in charge whips anyone who tires. Eventually, dizziness makes them all fall to the ground in ecstasy and convulsions, then, filled with the grace of the divine spirit, the couples unleash themselves upon each other with abandonment so that the liturgy ends with monstrous scenes of excess, lust and incest.

Rasputin's exorbitant nature predestined him to be filled with the divine spirit, and his exploits in these nocturnal orgies quickly made him popular, while at the same time his mystical gifts continued to develop. Going from village to village, he engaged in evangelical discussions and recited parables, then, little by little, he risked prophesying, carrying out exorcisms, and making incantations. He even boasted that he could pull off miracles and, for a hundred *versts* around Tobolsk, no one doubted his saintliness. Nevertheless, at this time, he had some annoying entanglements with the law for his peccadillos, such as his involvement in deceptions, rapes and abortions, and he would have come out of them badly if the ecclesiastical authorities had not already taken him under their protection.

In 1904, his renowned piety and the odor of his virtue reached St. Petersburg, and the notorious visionary, Father John of Kronstadt, who had consoled and sanctified Alexander III in his death agonies, wanted to meet this young Siberian prophet and received him at the monastery of St. Alexander Nevsky, congratulating himself on establishing, without any doubt, that Rasputin bore the marks of God Himself.

After this first appearance in the capital, Rasputin returned to Pokrovskoe, but from now on the horizons of his life were to widen considerably. He developed connections with a whole series of priests, some inspired, some charlatans, some scoundrels, of whom there were hundreds residing amid the foundations of the Russian clergy. This is how he gained, as an acolyte, Father Iliodor, an injurious and tempestuous monk, an erotic and a magician, adored by the people and a fierce enemy of liberals and Jews, who would later take over his monastery of Tsaritsin and hold the Sacred Synod at bay with the violence of his fanatical reactionary preaching.

Soon Grigory no longer contented himself with mixing with *moujiks* and the lesser clergy, and he was to be seen gravely accompanying higher priests, abbots, bishops and archimandrites who were all in agreement that they, like John of Kronstadt, could detect in him God's shining light, even while he frequently repulsed assaults from the Devil while also often succumbing to these same assaults.

At Tsaritsin, he deflowered a nun whom he had undertaken to exorcise. At Kazan, while drunk on a clear night in June, he was seen leaving a brothel, pushing before him a naked girl whom he was whipping with his belt, a scene that scandalized much of the town. In Tobolsk, he seduced the extremely pious wife of an engineer, Madame L....., and drove her so mad that she went about everywhere declaring her love for him and glorying in her shame. And it was she who initiated Rasputin in the refined delights of women of the world.

Through these non-stop exploits, his proclaimed sanctity grew day by day. People kneeled before him in the street, kissed his hands, and touched the hem of his robe, saying, "Our Christ, Our Savior, pray for us poor sinners! God will hear your prayers!" to which he would reply, "In the name of the Father, and of the Son, and of the Holy Ghost, I bless you, my little brothers. Be assured that Christ will soon return! Have patience in remembrance of his agony! Mortify your flesh because you love Him!"

In 1905, Bishop Feofan, the Inspector of the Theological Academy in St. Petersburg, a prelate of great piety and Confessor to the Empress, had the absurd inspiration to summon Rasputin so that he could observe at close range the wonderful effects of the grace present in the soul of this ingénue whom the demonic powers tormented so furiously.

His initial observations moved him to such ecstasies that, as a precaution, he submitted them to the judgment of several other bishops. One of these, Mgr. Hermogen, was venerated by all the clergy in Russia on account of his orthodoxy, the nobility of his character, and his customary asceticism. In secret, he was glorified for an admirable sacrifice he had made: wishing to rid himself of the temptations of the spirit and of the flesh, he had castrated himself, finding the courage to do so in the divine assurances transmitted to us by the Prophet Isaiah: "So the Lord said to the eunuchs, 'Those who strictly obey my law will receive a privileged place in my house. I will give them an exalted rank among my sons and daughters. I will give them an eternal name that will never die.' "

The scrupulous examination of Rasputin by Mgr. Hermogen led him to the same conclusions as Mgr. Feofan in relation to Rasputin's extraordinary gifts and his mysterious virtues as an apostolic healer.

Thanks to the endorsement of these two eminent priests, Rasputin now also gained favor with their many devoted followers, at the head of whom was one group of highly influential people: Grand Duke Nicholas Nikolaievich, Commander-in-Chief of the Imperial Guard; Grand Duke Nicholas' brother, Grand Duke Peter; and the wives of Grand Dukes Nicholas and Peter, Grand Duchesses Anastasia and Militza, daughters of the King of Montenegro. Grigory only had to make an appearance in order to astonish and fascinate this group of flighty and credulous souls who were much given to believing in the most ridiculous practices of magic, the occult and necromancy, and of all the mystical practitioners it was this Siberian prophet, this *Bojy tchelloviek*, whom they proclaimed as the "man of God."

The Montenegrin Grand Duchesses were notable for their tendency for admiration. Already, in 1900, they had introduced the magician Philippe of Lyon to the Russian court, and it was they who recommended Rasputin to the Emperor and Empress during the summer of 1906.

However, on the eve of their according him an audience, the Sovereigns hesitated and consulted Bishop Feofan, who assured them that, "Grigory Efimovich is a simple peasant, and only that. Your Majesties would benefit from hearing what he has to say because he gives voice to the soil of Russia that explains itself through the medium of his voice ... I know everything he is criticized for ... I know his sins ... They are innumerable and more often than not abominable. But, inside him, there is such a force of contrition and such a simple faith in heavenly suffering that I would almost guarantee his eternal salvation. After each time he repents, he is as pure as a child who has just been washed in baptismal water. God clearly favors him in his predilections ..."

A high officer of the court, the scion of one of the oldest names in Russia, Prince P....., had the sad honor of introducing, in secrecy, the obscene *moujik* to their Imperial Majesties. It was on a date that was both memorable and sinister in the annals of Russia, because, in addition to all the other profound problems that were undermining the Empire, now everyone would see the Tsar and Tsarina bring the throne to ruination with their own hands.

Chapter 8

From the day he entered the palace, Rasputin gained an extraordinary hold over the Sovereigns. And it wasn't because he flattered them. Absolutely not! Quite the opposite. From the first, he treated them harshly, with an audacious and overweening familiarity, and with a manner of address that was both trivial and colorful, which the Sovereigns, used to adulation and sated with flummery, took to be the "true voice of Russia."

All the court intriguers, and all those jockeying for their places in court, for titles and for paid imperial positions, naturally questioned what the source of his influence was. His modest lodgings in the Kirochnaia apartments, and later in the Anglisky Prospect, were soon besieged day and night by supplicants, generals, bureaucrats, bishops, archimandrites, imperial counsellors, senators, aide-de-camps, chamberlains, maids of honor, and women of the world, in an endless procession.

When he wasn't being detained by the Sovereigns or the Montenegrin Grand Duchesses, he was mostly to be found with Countess O....., who held salons for the champions of the Autocracy and the Orthodoxy. The highest dignitaries of the Church loved to meet there. Promotions in the church hierarchy, nominations to the Sacred Synod, and the most serious questions of dogma, discipline and liturgy were discussed in her presence. Her moral authority was recognized by everyone and proved a precious opportunity for Rasputin as she sometimes experienced heavenly visions.

One night, during a spiritual séance, St. Seraphim of Sarov, who had been canonized in 1903, appeared to her, and, lit up by a dazzling halo, declared, "There is a great prophet arrived among you. His mission is to reveal to the Tsar God's will and to guide him down the path of glory."

Countess O..... understood on the instant that he was referring to Rasputin.

The Emperor was powerfully struck by this oracle because, as the Head of the Church, he had taken a prominent and decisive role in the canonization of the blessed Seraphim and therefore held for him a particular level of devotion.

Amid the religious verbiage with which the *staretz* typically cloaked his eroticism, one idea surfaced above all: "We can only gain salvation through repentance. We must therefore sin in order to have the opportunity to repent. So, when God sends us temptation, we must give in to it as a necessary precondition for a fruitful repentance. The first word that Christ brought down to man in life and in truth, was it not 'Repent!'? But how can you repent if you have not already sinned?"

His standard homilies were full of ingenious perorations on the salutary value of tears and the redeeming virtue of contrition. One of his favorite arguments, and the one that worked best on the women in his audience, was, "What most often stops us from sinning isn't the fear of sinning; because, if we truly feared sinning, we wouldn't be tempted by it. Do you ever want to eat food that disgusts you? No. What stops us sinning, and frightens us about sinning, is how the thought of penitence affronts our pride. Perfect contrition requires perfect humility. However, we don't want to humble ourselves, even in front of God. That is the whole secret of why we resist temptation. But the Lord Our Judge is not fooled, and when we find ourselves in the valley of Josaphat, he will remind us of all the opportunities for salvation that he has given us and that we have spurned ..."

In the second Christian century, these beliefs were already professed by a Phrygian sect. The heretic Montanus complacently declared them in front of his beautiful lady friends of Laodicea, and they obtained for him much the same outcomes as they did for Rasputin ...

There has been much discussion as to whether this Siberian peasant was sincere in claiming to have supernatural powers or whether he wasn't, at base, merely a charlatan and a fraud. Opinion has always been more or less divided because the *staretz* was always replete with contrasts, inconsistencies and bizarre affectations.

The laws of Psychology, or at least many a psychological experiment, argue for his sincerity ... for his complete sincerity. He could not possibly have exercised such an overwhelming fascination for people if he wasn't personally convinced of his own extraordinary gifts. And it was his faith in his mystical powers that was the principal force in his rise to prominence. He was the first to be fooled by his own words and practices.

And there is some support for this proposition. The Grand Master of the hermit phenomenon in the sixteenth century, the ingenious author of 'Philosophia Sagax,' Paracelsus, already correctly assessed that the persuasive force behind a magician must necessarily emanate from his own belief in his dynamism. "Non potest facere quod non credit posse facere" [You cannot achieve that which you do not believe you can achieve].

Besides, how could Rasputin possibly doubt that an exceptional force came from him when each day he was confronted by the proof of the belief his entourage had in him? When he claimed to be inspired by God to impose his fantasies on the Empress, her immediate obedience demonstrated the truth in his claim. It was a question of reciprocal reinforcement.

In modern psychiatry, Rasputin personifies to an extreme the classic personality type of the "erotic and religious myth spinner."

We know that the phenomenon of the "myth spinner" is a product of the brain indicating abnormal and incessant activity with regard to the creative imagination. Individuals afflicted with this pathological condition have a personality and play a role that they animate, maintain and continually enrich with a prodigious fertility of the imagination, with an astonishing mastery in the combining of lies and sincerity, of illusion with desire.

This is why, from the start of the century, Rasputin believed himself to be in direct contact with God, Jesus Christ, the Virgin Mary, the archangels and the saints. From this point, he put together a fantastical story that he manifested until he could no longer separate it from his real life.

The mystical foundations and suggestibility that can be found among all Russians additionally offered him a wonderful terrain to reinforce his confabulations.

Finally, we can add one psychological perversion that can frequently be observed among spinners of myths: lubricious sensuality – the driving, irresistible, and insatiable obsession with overweening sexuality.

Chapter 9

Around this time, the Tsarevich was suffering greatly from his hemophilia. With the least injury, and sometimes without even that, he would start to bleed, and, despite all medical attention, would continue to bleed for several days in a row, inflicting atrocious pain on the poor little one. Agonized by this display of the total powerlessness of official medicine, his parents turned to the hazy and miraculous solutions that Rasputin had to offer.

When brought to the child's bedside, the *Bojy tchelloviek*, the "man of God," never hesitated, and he appeared neither embarrassed nor humbled like "those idiot doctors." Rather, in a firm voice, he would recite a bizarre prayer resembling a magical incantation. Then, with an air of lofty self-confidence, he would continue on.

And the most extraordinary thing about all this was that, in most cases, the crisis would soon be brought to an end and the bleeding would stop. It was probably due to mere coincidence, but the Emperor and Empress never had any doubt that this Siberian peasant had supernatural powers at his disposal, furnished by a heavenly will.

In his new role, Rasputin decided that it would be best for him to recruit as a collaborator a man no less of an eccentric and a charlatan than himself, the healer Badmaiev. He was a Mongol and a Buryat who had escaped from the monasteries of Tibet. He lacked a university education and he practiced medicine, or rather sorcery, only in secret. Nevertheless, he commanded a strong, if mysterious, reputation in St. Petersburg, and patients flooded into his clinic on the Liteiny Prospect while the police looked the other way because of his powerful connections.

Bolstered by his ignorance and his claimed enlightenment, Badmaeiv did not hesitate to take on the most difficult and abstruse cases in the world of medicine, although he had a particular interest in nervous illnesses and those related to the female physiology.

He created for himself a secret pharmacopeia, giving his treatments flamboyant names and selling what amounted to narcotics, tranquilizers, anesthetics, menstrual stimulants and aphrodisiacs to a vulnerable public. Some of the names of his medicines included 'Elixir of Tibet,' 'Powder of Nirvritti,' 'Flowers of Ashoka,' 'Balm of Nyen-Tchen,' 'Essence of Black Lotus,' and many more, although, in truth, he simply relabeled drugs that he had bought from a local pharmacy where he had an accomplice.

From the time of their first joint consultation with the Tsarevich at his bedside, the two men understood each other and joined forces, while the formal scientific community placed discretion over valor and bowed to their preeminence.

Meanwhile, the saner elements of St. Petersburg society hummed with all the scandals that were being disseminated about the *Staretz* of Pokrovskoe, and eventually a great howl of indignation swelled up from everywhere over the frequency of his visits to the imperial palace, his self-confessed role in many arbitrary and contentious orders of the Sovereigns, the outrageous effrontery of his behavior, and his shameless and cynical morality.

Despite rigorous official censorship, the press took to denouncing the ignominious acts of the Siberian healer, while carefully avoiding going so far as to impugn the reputations of the Sovereigns themselves, although everyone could read between the lines as to what was really being said.

Realizing that it might be better if he disappeared for a while, the "man of God" decided in March 1911 to visit Jerusalem. This unexpected decision filled his disciples with both sadness and admiration, because only a saintly soul could respond so nobly to such vile gossip, and, as is often the case, distance only served to increase his prestige.

The sublime poetry of the sanctuaries he visited and the care with which he observed his devotions did not distract him from remembering his admirers in St. Petersburg, and he wrote to them often. His correspondents took many pains to read his letters because his illiterate writing style meant that no one could decipher more than a quarter of the words he had scrawled across the page. But when they finally made sense of this gobbledygook, oh what sweetness, what enchantment and what wisdom they discovered within!

Having a sincere faith and a lively imagination, long accustomed to discussing the mysteries of mysticism, and, like all Russian peasants, fully cognizant of the seductiveness inherent in subtleties of expression, Rasputin skillfully navigated the picturesque language of addresses, parables and homilies.

Here, for instance, are some of the things he wrote from Jerusalem:

> Let us pity the malicious and the perfidious, the rapacious and the ambitious, because they cannot see the sun, because they stumble along in eternal night, because they receive no consolation from the beauty of the spring!

> What foolishness it is to celebrate a cult by emphasizing magnificence! Isn't a poverty of spirit infinitely superior to this? In God's eyes, gold counts for nothing. The people are not fooled. This is why God loves all the sects because only there is the poverty of the spirit venerated ...

> What I felt standing in front of Our Lord's tomb was ineffable. It was as if I was standing in front of a great hall of love. I wanted to kiss the whole world and in each man I espied a saint. Great love is blind to human imperfections ...

Soon the Empress and Mme. Vyrubov begged him to return because they had great need of his illuminating presence, but all their urgings had no effect on him, and, when he returned to Russia, he decided to spend a relaxing time on the Volga in the company of his friend and fellow-scoundrel Iliodor.

However, on September 15, he was abruptly torn away from his frolic in the countryside by a telegram from Alexandra Feodorovna recalling him urgently to Kiev where the President of the Council, Stolypin, had just been assassinated under the very eyes of the Sovereigns.

This drama had taken place in the theater during a gala performance that the Emperor and Empress were honoring with their presence. The Okhrana had already been on the scent of the plot for several days, the details becoming clearer by the hour thanks to the efforts of a young Jewish lawyer, Bogrov, who was linked to several terrorist organizations, and whose sudden change of heart had allowed him to be hired as an informer by the imperial police.

Immediately, sinister rumors spread around the city. Several times, and at the last minute, the official itinerary of the Sovereigns had been changed, although, warned of the situation, Nicholas II had remained his usual calm and fatalistic self. No less courageous, Alexandra Feodorovna forced herself to maintain her serenity during her official engagements because a tragic presentiment, a clear intuition of an invisible menace, pulled cruelly at her heart strings.

On the evening of September 14, when President of the Council Stolypin arrived at the theater, one of his female friends shouted out, "Tell me, Peter Arkadievich, what is that decoration, that great cross of enamel and rubies that you wear on your uniform?"

"It's the highest honor of the Red Cross," he replied.

"Ah! I don't like it," his interlocutor announced with a shiver. "It frightens me. It looks to me like the cross of a martyr."

During the second intermission, Stolypin was standing in the orchestra section in front of the imperial box, when a well turned out young man, wearing the regulation black tie and evening dress, casually approached him and pumped three bullets from his revolver straight into his chest.

The victim was thrown backward into his seat, then, turning toward the Emperor, he blessed him with the sign of the cross, raising his head to say, "I am content to die for Your Majesty."

The police seized the assassin and dragged him out of the room, whereupon, while searching him and interrogating him, they were astonished to discover that he was an agent of the Okhrana, the very one who had been keeping them informed of the details of the plot.

"It's Bogrov!" they exclaimed.

In reaction to this drama, the next day Alexandra Feodorvna started suffering violently from heart spasms and nervous derangement.

What particulary affected her spirit was that the police, despite their apparent preparedness, despite their having doubled up on their precautions, and despite their foreknowledge of the plot, had failed to prevent the assassination from taking place. Worse, the assassin had been able to enter the theater and approach his victim because he was a vetted member of the Okhrana. This proof of powerlessness and fatality, the implacable course of this tragedy – did it not suggest that it was carried out according to the resolute will of God?

On the other hand, the haloed face of her Friend shone out before her eyes like an icon as she summoned him in her distress, because she was beginning to understand something that she would never doubt again: that only the prayers of the *staretz* could reach God through the intercession of Our Lord Jesus Christ and ensure the safety of the imperial family and the saintly motherland of Russia.

Chapter 10

Having miraculously calmed down the Empress and recognized beyond doubt his unlimited power over her, Rasputin returned to St. Petersburg nine months after leaving it for Jerusalem, and immediately the orgies, the insanities and the ignominies returned as well.

But already a certain amount of dissension was surfacing among the ranks of his followers: Some considered him compromising and far too libidinous; others worried about his growing influence over Church and State.

In particular, the ecclesiastical world was still recovering from a shameful nomination deriving from the weakness of the Emperor, when Rasputin obtained the Bishopric of Tobolsk for his childhood friend, an illiterate peasant, a man who was vulgar in all senses of the word, Father Varnava. At the same time it was learned that the Supreme Procurator of the Sacred Synod had been ordered to confer a priesthood on Rasputin.

This time, all hell broke loose.

On December 29, Mgr. Hermogen, the Bishop of Saratov, the monk Iliodor, and several priests had an altercation with the *staretz*. They insulted him and pushed him around, calling him, "Accursed! Sacrilegious! Fornicator! Disgusting beast! Devil's serpent!" To end it all, they spat in his face.

Initially caught off-balance, and pinned against the wall, Grigory replied by vomiting out a litany of injustices against him. To this, Hermogen, a very large and powerful man, hit him violently over the head with the cross he wore across his chest, screaming, "Get down on your knees, you miserable sinner! Get down on your knees in front of the icons of the saints! Beg for God's pardon for all your filthy ways! Swear that you will never again infect the palace of our beloved Tsar with your repulsive presence!"

Rasputin, trembling with fear and bleeding from the nose, struck his chest, stammered out some prayers, and promised never to appear before the Emperor again. Finally he was released to a bombardment of insults and spitting.

As soon as he had fled this trap, Rasputin ran to the court at Tsarskoe Selo, and it didn't take him long to relish the joys of vengeance.

A few days later, the Supreme Procurator ordered the Sacred Synod to elevate Mgr. Hermogen to a bishopric and exiled him to the monastery of Khirovitsy in Lithuania. As for the monk Iliodor, seized by the police, he was incarcerated in the monastic penitentiary of Floristchevo, near Vladimir.

Early on, the police found themselves unable to keep a lid on the scandal. Speaking in front of the Duma, the Head of the Octobrist Party, Gutchkov, denounced in veiled terms the relationship between Rasputin and the court. As for Moscow, the religious and moral center of the Empire, the most qualified and respected of the interpreters of Orthodox Slavism – Count Cheremetiev, Novosilov, Droujinin, and Vasnetsov – protested publicly against the servile attitude of the Sacred Synod, even calling for a National Council to reform the Church.

Bishop Feofan, who had finally seen the light about the "man of God," and who held himself responsible for having introduced him to the court, also worthily spoke out against him, and the Sacred Synod duly reassigned him to the Tauride Palace, despite his being the Empress' confessor.

The Presidency of the Council remained in Kokovtsov's hands. He was also the Minister of Finance. As a man of integrity and courage, he tried all he could to educate the Emperor as to Rasputin's true nature, begging him on March 1, 1912, to authorize him to send the *staretz* back to the village where he was born.

"This man has abused the confidence of the Empress," he declared. "He is a charlatan and a chancer of the worst sort, and he has excited public opinion against him. The newspapers …"

The Emperor interrupted his minister with a disdainful smile.

"You pay attention to the newspapers?"

"Yes, Sire, I pay attention to them when they attack my sovereign and the reputation of the dynasty. And nowadays it is the most loyal newspapers that are the most severe in their criticism …"

Annoyed, the Emperor interrupted him again.

"Their complaints are absurd. I hardly know Rasputin."

Kokovtsov hesitated before continuing, but continued anyway.

"Sire, in the name of your family, in the name of your heirs, I beg you to allow me to take the necessary measures to return Rasputin to his village forever."

The Emperor responded coldly, "I will tell him myself to leave and never to return."

"Do I take this for a final decision, Your Majesty?"

"Yes, this is my decision," he confirmed. Then, glancing at the clock that was showing that it was 12:30, the Emperor held out his hand to Kokovtsov. "Goodbye, Vladimir Nikolaievich. I will not keep you any longer."

At four o'clock the same day, Rasputin telephoned Senator S....., an intimate friend of Kokovtsov, and bawled at him in an aggrieved voice, "Your friend the President tried this morning to frighten Papa. He tried to blacken my name any way he could. But he failed utterly. Papa and Mama still love me. You can tell Vladimir Nikolaievich that."

On May 6, all the ministers got together in formal attire at the imperial palace to offer their congratulations for the Empress' birthday, but when Alexandra Feodorovna passed by Kokovstov, she turned her back on him.

Several days beforehand, the *staretz* had left for Tobolsk, not because he had been ordered to do so, but because he wished to see what was happening in his little household in Pokrovskoe. While in the process of leaving, he had savagely pronounced a terrifying warning.

"I know that the Pharisees are after me. Don't listen to them! If you abandon me, you will lose your son and your crown within six months."

The Empress replied, "How could we abandon you? Are you not our only friend, our only savior from those who would do us harm, our intercessor and witness before God?"

Then, throwing herself to her knees, the Empress asked for his blessing.

On September 7, 1912, Russia celebrated the anniversary of a great and historic event, the Battle of Borodino, that rallied the nation, although Napoleon called it by a more resonant name – the "Battle for Moscow."

In truth, both sides could have justifiably declared victory because, if the Russian army under Kutusov had got the better of the French army for the first time and inflicted horrendous casualties on it, the French army had still managed to enter Moscow, the most sacred city of Russia, a few days later.

The 1912 celebrations severely tested Alexandra Feodorovna's constitution. The cruel tightening around her temples, the bitter contraction of her mouth, the wild palpitations of her heart, the jangling of her nerves, the sudden red blotching to her face, widespread and continuous anxiety, vertigo, and dizziness rendered each ceremony intolerable for her.

Nicholas II pressed her to travel with him to Poland after the celebrations were over. Their destination was the beautiful palace of Spala, surrounded by an immensely wild and silent forest. There they spent a peaceful family holiday until the second half of October. Then, one day, the little Tsarevich, while returning from rowing around the lake, misjudged his lunge for the shore and struck his thigh against the jetty.

Initially, the damage was considered only minor, however, the next day, a swelling appeared in his groin and his thigh immediately blew up as his temperature rose precipitously. Doctors were hastily summoned from St. Petersburg and Moscow, and diagnosed him as having a blood clot that was already infected and required instant surgery, except that the Tsarevich's hemophilia rendered such a course of action hazardous in the extreme.

The patient's temperature rose inexorably by the hour and on October 21 it reached 39.8C. His desperate parents refused to leave his bedside because his doctors feared for the worst. In the church at Spala, the priests set up continuous prayers day and night. At the same time in Moscow, the Emperor ordered a solemn liturgy of healing to take place in front of the icon of the miraculous Virgin of Iverskaia, and from morning to night the people of St. Petersburg filed into Our Lady of Kazan.

On October 22, there was no improvement and the patient's temperature had risen to 40C. That morning, several high officials, including Foreign Minister Sazonov, came to make their regular reports to the Emperor, but had to wait for a long time for an audience because the Emperor would not tear himself away from his son.

Suddenly, the door of the salon opened to the sound of two knocks and the Empress entered the room.

She was pale, emaciated and tragic-looking, and yet she was also smiling.

She responded calmly to the anxious enquiries that were put to her.

"The doctors can still not see any improvement in his condition, but I personally have no fear. Last night I received a telegram from Father Grigory that has given me complete reassurance." Then she proceeded to read the telegram at the top of her voice. "God has seen your tears and heard your prayers. Do not concern yourself anymore. Your son will live."

The next day, on October 23, the Tsarevich's temperature dropped to 38.9C. Two days later, the blood clot disappeared and Alexei was saved.

Chapter 11

Rather than releasing Alexandra Feodorovna from the full force of her nervous disposition, this miracle only drove her on, without respite, to yet more religious fervor, to a blind and trembling submission of her thoughts, of her beliefs, of her desires, of her strength, of her being, before the mercy of Rasputin. And, to the misfortune of Russia, Nicholas II followed her, by some sort of contagion, into the same level of bedevilment.

Thus, from 1913, the Siberian healer began to exercise an influence, directly and indirectly, openly and covertly, on the governance of the State.

Until now, his role either at court or in social circles amounted to nothing more than sardonic remarks and scandalous behavior. The madness was not yet fully up to speed.

Now, the *Bojy tchelloviek*, the "man of God," turned his attention to politics, or rather politics turned their attention on him.

By the fact alone that he spent time with the Sovereigns at all hours, by the fact that he shone so brightly in their eyes, by the fact that they attributed to him a divine mission, by the fact that he could issue injunctions and reproaches to them personally during intimate conversations with unheard-of abandon, by the fact that he was a diabolical charlatan in every aspect of his being, he necessarily became a factor in the exercise of extreme power.

It was the fundamental tenet of tsarism that the Emperor held, by the grace of God, unlimited power, and that his orders were peremptory, unchallengeable and not subject in any way to any right of appeal.

This resulted in the timid and feeble Duma exercising, in practice, virtually no control in the political arena; in the press only having the right to remain silent; and in the police, with all their enormous prerogatives, reinforced by the terrifying threat of being sent to a prison in Siberia, merely condoning and covering up the worst of Rasputin's abuses.

The whole of national life, as much in private as in public, was enveloped by the unbreakable structure of the Autocracy and the Orthodoxy. The master of the Emperor, and especially the master of his religious conscience, was therefore the master of the occult within the Empire.

The *staretz* soon realized that a burgeoning clientele of influential people was rapidly forming around him, keen to tie their future and their fortunes to his.

The most redoubtable of these was the Minister of the Interior, Nicholas Maklakov, whose accommodating and fawning submissiveness was most pleasing to the Sovereigns. Almost equally important was the Minister of Justice, Scheglovitov, the leader of the Extreme Right in the Council of the Empire, and relentless defender of tsarism in its totality, who put at the service of his ideas a lively spirit, incisive oratory, and a bludgeoning manner. After him there was the Procurator-General of the Sacred Synod, Vladimir Sabler, a despicable and servile character through whom Rasputin would ultimately gain the devotion of all the highest members of the clergy, both monastic and secular. Then there were Admiral Nilov (the Emperor's General Aide-de-Camp), Stürmer (the Master of the Court), Dobrovolsky (the Procurator of the Senate), and the extremely powerful and cunning Director of Police, Bieletzky.

Up against this nefarious claque stood several men of outstanding pride and courage, such as Kokovtsov (the President of the Council), Sazonov (the Foreign Minister), and Prince Orlov (the Head of the Imperial Military Chancellery), who voluntarily exposed themselves to the covert hostility of Nicholas II and the open hostility of Alexandra Feodorovna, although they were supported by the entire imperial family.

The Dowager-Empress, Marie Feodorovna, the pure and noble Grand Duchess Elisabeth Feodorovna (the sister of the Empress), and Marie Pavlovna (the Emperor's aunt) had tried many times to open the Sovereigns' eyes to the abject behavior of the *staretz*, but each time they were told drily, "We won't offend our pious friend by defending him. Are not the saints always subjected to calumnies?"

In the annals of the Romanovs, the year of 1913 marked a centenary that was much more worthy of celebration than 1912, as it referred to the establishment of the Romanov dynasty itself, the impetuous outburst of patriotism that miraculously saved Russia in the spring of 1613 by elevating the young Michael Romanov to the throne in Moscow.

For the previous fifteen years, and especially since the tragic death of Boris Godunov, the Empire of the Tsars flailed around in a horrific torment. The capital, the sacred Moscow, was in the hands of the hated Poles, with all its provinces subjected to pillage, massacres and devastation. The whole political and social edifice had collapsed, and the key families were either destroyed or in flight.

No hope was left in the Russian soul, no strength was left in their hearts, and it seemed that Russia would be condemned to an eternity in the shadows of barbarity.

The priests in the Kremlin sorrowfully asked themselves whether the curse Jehovah placed on Babylon had not been renewed on Moscow: "I will make of this land an immense desert, a pile of ruins stretching into eternity."

Then, in the spring of 1613, a sudden awakening of the people was provoked by an obscure boyar called Pojarsky and a humble merchant called Minine, and a sense of national consciousness was reestablished.

Within a few months, Moscow was liberated, the Poles were driven off, public order was restored, and at last the whole grandiose heritage of Ivan the Terrible was rebuilt and reanimated under the scepter of Michael Romanov.

This was the most decisive hour that the Russian people had lived through since the heroic times of St. Vladimir. After this, Russia joined modern civilization, a process driven even faster by Peter the Great and Catherine the Great. From this point, a new power weighed down on the destiny of Europe and Asia, an enormous, exuberant and idealistic power, convinced that here below it was the instrument of the divine will.

And yet it was also an adventurous, undisciplined and chimeric power, as formidable for its overwhelming enthusiasms as for the wildness of its dreams, the suddenness of its changes of direction, and the explosive violence of its reactions.

In order to commemorate "the divine miracle" of 1613, Nicholas II ordered up a long series of splendid events to take place throughout the Empire that would reaffirm, in the eyes of his people and of the world, the enormity of the achievements of the Romanov dynasty. The centerpiece of this program was a symbolic pilgrimage to be made by the Sovereigns in the Volga region, where the national renewal had begun. They would therefore give thanks to God in Vladimir, Nizhny Novgorod, Kostroma, Iarolslavl, and Rostov, before finishing up in Moscow.

From May 29 to June 10, a series of solemn and superb spectacles took place from town to town under a radiant sky, reminding everyone, yet again, that the Autocracy and the Orthodoxy were inextricably intertwined, in that they were all marked by religious ceremonies and celebrations.

While the imperial progress continued up and down the Volga, the *moujiks* in their hundreds of thousands pressed forward on bended knees, accompanied by their priests, their crosses, their standards, their banners and their icons, all as one chanting hymns, raising their hands to heaven, ravished and enraptured by a common ecstasy, ardently blessing their Sovereigns.

In the towns where the heroic drama of 1613 had taken place, the enthusiasm of the crowds spilled over at the magnificence of the procession, the salvoes of the artillery, and the bursts of church bells, and expressed itself in tumultuous acclaim. In Kostromoa, in front of the legendary monastery of Ipatiev, where Michael Romanov had accepted the crown of the Autocracy from the Moscow delegation, the fervor of those present took a turn toward the delirious and the frenetic.

The symbolic pilgrimage ended in Moscow, on June 10, in a flamboyant apotheosis.

How many times did the Tsar and Tsarina say to their entourage, "The people love us! Look how the people love us!"?

And it was true. Seeing the Sovereigns in all their sanctified splendor moved the conscience of the people, of the masses, of the most humble. But in higher society, among the bourgeoisie and the nobility, many a frown crossed their brows, many critical words, many ill-intentioned criticisms, and all these directed mercilessly at the Empress.

For one thing, during several ceremonies – and not just those of a lesser importance – she was absent. Why wasn't she next to the Emperor? Was she ill? Clearly not, because she had given the impression of perfect health when she had disembarked from the imperial train.

What the public couldn't have known was that, just before making an appearance at the ceremony, the poor woman was seized by thunderous shooting pains, convulsive spasms, and sudden attacks of dizziness, after which she had to be led quietly away.

In the same vein, one night in Moscow during a magically spectacular ball, she became frozen in her haughty reserve and upset those persons of refinement who had been accorded the privilege of meeting her. However, that particular night, she happened to be suffering from one of her most painful illnesses, a nervous and paralyzing exhaustion, a sort of mental eclipse that rendered her incapable of speaking even as she attempted to mouth the words.

In truth, she was reproached by a much more serious criticism, which was sadly well merited. Had she not committed the inexcusable mistake of wanting Rasputin to accompany her at each stage of their progress, so that, in these magnificent times, she could feel his sweet intimacy constantly wrapping itself around her?

People everywhere observed with astonishment that she barely bothered to hide the presence of this obscene *moujik*, and this fuelled their outrage against the Empress.

After the debilitating grind of this long series of celebratory rituals, the Sovereigns took time off for several weeks among the charming fjords of the coast of Finland on their yacht, The Standart,

Then, on August 4, the annual grand military maneuvers at Krasnoe-Selo began, where Nicholas II hosted General Joffre, who had come to point out the increasing threat being posed to France and Russia by the rapid build-up of German armaments.

On August 20, the imperial family moved on to Livadia in the Crimea with the intention of staying until Christmas. There, under the restorative influence of azure-blue skies, brightly-lit horizons, sea breezes, and luxurious vegetation, Alexandra Feodorovna daily recovered her calm and caught up on her sleep, endowed with a sense of serenity and balance that she had not known for so long.

But what enchanted her the most was that, a mere three kilometers away, in the Bay of Yalta, Mme. Vyrubova and Rasputin had set up their own residences.

By a cruel irony, that year of 1913, which was supposed to represent the magnificent apogee of the Romanov dynasty, in fact delivered it a harm from which it would never recover.

According to those historians who have studied this period, this was the year that Rasputin perniciously made his entrance onto the political scene by forming around the Empress a despicable and all-powerful claque, a "camarilla"; and this was the year that saw a final rift between those who stood for all that was sane in Russian society and political affairs, and those who were merely intriguers, sharks and charlatans, and yet who would come to personify the imperial court itself.

Daily discussions inevitably centered around the credulousness of the Emperor, and inflammatory gossip was ceaselessly put about regaling the sordid secret life of the palace, taking on a robustly scandalous and corrosive life of its own in undermining the underpinnings of the regime, and, in short, dealing a mortal blow to the traditions of tsarist

Orthodoxy that lay at the very heart of the edifice of the Russian state.

Chapter 12

In 1914, war broke out, but what were the Empress' thoughts about this?

I saw her and chatted with her during those tragic times. I even had a long talk with her in Moscow when the Emperor and all his family came to pray before the relics of the saints during those great ceremonies that took place at the Kremlin. And I assure you that, without hesitation, she was entirely at one with the Emperor in her thoughts, in her conscience and in her patriotism. She supported him with all her might, while time after time he appealed to Kaiser Wilhelm II for there to be a peaceful solution. Until the final moment, she begged him to pursue negotiations with Germany and Austria, to attempt the impossible in avoiding this catastrophe that threatened the entire world.

And when Kaiser Wilhelm's crime was consummated, she had but one thought: to arouse the Russian people to do all they could to bring this war to a victorious conclusion.

On this issue – and whatever anyone says – she remained firm. She never even considered that Russia should sue for peace, any more than the Emperor did, before Germany was brought to its knees and it was agreed by all the allies that the war should be brought to an end.

When the Empress saw the level of cruelty and barbarism that Germany chose to employ in fighting the war, she was filled with an indignant rage. Speaking of the bombardment of Reims with her aunt, Grand Duchess Maria Pavlovna, she said, "What a sacrilege, what an outrage it is to bombard Reims Cathedral! The Germans have lost all sense of morality and Christian duty!"

Indeed, she supported all that France did, for its passion, for its poise and for its tenacity, displaying a warm admiration for Russia's ally that she frequently expressed directly to me. I therefore have the right and the duty to repeat to you that, throughout the war, even when Russia was facing its worst defeats, even when Russian public opinion lost any desire for victory and abandoned itself to the deepest pessimism, even when the specter of revolution arose from all quarters, Alexandra Feodorovna held her head high and remained steadfast of heart. Nor did she ever allow to be said in her presence what, alas, I heard only too often, that Russia should desert its allies and conclude a hurried peace in order to avoid any further catastrophes.

So, where did the odious stories that surrounded the Empress and so brutally tarnished her memory come from?

This was indeed a curious phenomenon, one that was more psychological than political in its essence, and unfortunately for her, its origin was in her relationship with Rasputin.

During those tragic weeks of July and August 1914, Rasputin was absent from St. Petersburg.

On June 16, he had just arrived in his village of Pokrovskoe in Siberia when he fell victim to a mundane misadventure from which all his supernatural powers and all his magical forces were insufficient to protect him.

One fine day, a prostitute from Tobolsk, Chionya Guseva, offered to sell him her services, an offer which he declined, and so she plunged a knife into his guts, shouting, "I have just killed the Antichrist!"

Then she tried to kill herself.

Twenty-six years of age and pretty, this girl was completely typical of Russian prostitutes, being the victim of hysteria, alcoholism and mysticism all at the same time. She could well have fallen out of the pages of a book by Tolstoy or Dostoyevsky.

For almost a month, this "saintly man" hovered between life and death. The Empress, overwrought, immediately rushed to him the best surgeon St. Petersburg could provide and she telegraphed him daily.

Finally, he started to recover toward the end of July, while the diplomatic crisis that would lead to a world war was breaking out. Yet he instantly saw what was happening, thanks to his mysterious instinct for divination and his incomprehensible and dazzling ability in the art of prophecy, of which he had furnished so many examples, violently proclaiming himself to be against the war.

He even graced the Emperor with his opinion.

My dear friend, I tell you once again, a terrifying cloud is spreading itself over Russia. Horror! Unimaginable suffering!

It grows dark from every quarter and I see no light of hope emerging on the horizon.

Everywhere there are tears, an ocean of tears! And as for blood …? I cannot find the words! The horror is indescribable.

Nonetheless, I know that everything depends on you.

Those who wish for war fail to understand that it will be our loss. Heavy will be the punishment of the heavens when God will deprive us of all reason, because it will be the beginning of the end.
You are the Tsar, the Father of your people. Don't let fools triumph and perish alongside their people! Yes, we will conquer Germany, but what will become of Russia? In all truth, I tell you: despite our victory, there will never have been, since the beginning of time, a more terrible martyrdom than will be suffered by the Russian people. Russia will drown in blood and her loss will be total.

With immense sadness!

Grigory.

That Nicholas II was moved by so terrible and eloquent a prediction is without doubt, but in the face of the warlike preparations of the German forces, and in face of the implacable desire for war emanating from Berlin and Vienna, how could he have avoided this catastrophe?

On July 29, he personally telegraphed Kaiser Wilhelm in the friendliest of terms, proposing to submit the grievance between Austria and Serbia to the court of arbitration in The Hague, but the self-absorbed Kaiser did not deign to honor him with a reply.

By the middle of September, Rasputin had recovered from his injuries and returned to Petrograd, and, his eyes full of passion and fresh of face, he seemed more vigorous and swashbuckling than ever, to the delight of his claque.

When this "saintly" friend arrived at the palace of Peterhof, he was greeted with hosannas! Everyone hugged and blessed each other, and the *staretz* wasted no time in claiming before the Sovereigns that his recovery was striking proof of his divine protection because the doctors had predicted that he would die.

He spoke of the war, but in careful terms. While he did not retract his shocking predictions, nor did he seek to explain himself with any clarity, cloaking his thoughts in vague aphorisms and enigmatic sentences, his instincts telling him that this was not the time to express pessimism.

Since the start of the war, a great spirit had arisen among the Russian people. In Moscow, Iaroslavl, Kazan, Toula, Kiev, Kharkov, Odessa, Rostov, Samara, Tiflis, Orenbourg, Tomsk and Irkoutsk, everywhere there was the same enthusiasm, the same grave and pious passion, the same rallying around the Tsar, the same belief in victory, and the same arousal of the national consciousness. No one opposed the war and the terrible days of 1905 seemed to have been erased from all memories. The soul of sacred Russia had not been so vividly expressed since the sacred days of 1812.

At the front, the armies were admirable in their vigor and commitment, fighting the Germans with a surprisingly heroic, supple and tenacious persistence. As for the Austrians, the Russian armies battered them relentlessly, and quickly forced them to abandon Galicia, where once the princes of Kiev had ruled. On the French side, the Battle of the Marne had just ruined Germany's phantasmagoric reputation for invincibility.

Better still, those infidels the Turks, long committed to the cause of the German powers, now dared to attack Russia, immediately lending the war a new, sure and evident significance to the souls of the Russian people. All the romantic utopias of Orthodox nationalism, all the infinite dreams of messianic Slavism, all the blinding and fiery apocalypses that had for four centuries – since the marriage of Ivan III and Sophie Paléologue – taken root in popular consciousness, all these foolish imaginations took flight at once. There was no doubt about it: the time had come for the eagle of the Tsars to flutter over a purified Byzantium where the cross of the Savior would shine out anew over the cupola of St. Sophie.

In Moscow, in the burning atmosphere that shines over the Kremlin, they repeatedly sang the famous song of the poet Tyutchev:

Moscow, the city of Peter,
And the city of Constantin,
There are the three sacred capitals
Of the Russian Empire.

But where are the frontiers
To the north and to the east,
To the south and to the west?
Destiny will reveal
Where they are in the future.

Seven seas in the hinterland
And seven great rivers;
From the Nile to the Neva,
From the Elba to the China,
From the Volga to the Euphrates,
From the Ganges to the Danube –
There is the Russian Empire
And it will last for all the centuries!
The Holy Spirit predicts it
And Daniel prophesied it!

Rasputin was too cunning not to sense the spirit of the times: It was not the time to fulminate against the war; that would come all too soon.

The year of 1914 ended under unhappy circumstances. Each day the war seemed far longer, far harder and far more murderous than had been expected.

Then, as in 1904 and 1905, there started to be open criticism of all the weaknesses, all the corruption, all the dishonesty and all the underlying rot of the government.

There were frequent failures on the front caused by the imperiousness of the high command; the scarcity of transport; the inexplicable absence of rifles, of field guns and of shells; the incompetence of the machinery of administration; the ballooning of the economic crisis; and the quiet fomenting of revolutionary thinking.

All of this evaded the censor and broke out into open day, worrying and depressing the general public.

And once again there appeared that lamentable weakness of the Russian character – the rush to despair and recrimination.

That astute psychologist and powerful spinner of tales, Chekov, forcefully described this several years earlier: "Why," he said, "do we give up so quickly? How is it that, after expending so much ardor, passion and faith at the outset, we then collapse? And, when we fall, why do we never try to rise again?"

Nevertheless, the *staretz* didn't hesitate to declaim to whoever would listen, "If that bitch Chionya Guseva hadn't slashed me with a filthy knife in the stomach, I would have saved the peace! All I would have needed to have done was to have looked Nicholas fully in the eye and said to him, 'Do what you like, but let there be no war! Do you understand me?' "

And his greatest admirers were also claiming to whoever would listen, "If our saintly friend had not been incapacitated and stranded so far away from us during July, we would have been spared this war. God guides him, while the ministers commit every mistake they can think of and have fallen into every trap. Oh, it's a tragedy that he wasn't here to open the Emperor's eyes!"

However, in front of the Sovereigns, the *staretz* chose his words more carefully as he saw that they were completely enraged by Germany, completely determined to prosecute the war with determination and energy, and completely sure of final victory, therefore judging it wise to rein in his thunderous eloquence.

I saw this myself one day in the February of 1915.

Rasputin had expressed his desire several times to meet me in secret at the house of one of his admirers, but he seemed so repugnant and so compromising that I evaded his advances.

Subsequently, I was told that it would greatly please Her Majesty the Empress if I would agree to get to know her pious friend. I therefore agreed to meet him, as if by chance, in a salon where he was much admired.

While I was chatting with my hostess, Countess H....., the door burst open loudly and a tall man, wearing the type of long, black caftan that *moujiks* wear on high days and holidays, and heavy boots, advanced with great strides towards our hostess, whom he proceeded to hug noisily.

It was the *staretz*.

Throwing a brief glance in my direction, he asked, "Who are you?"

I gave him my name.

"Ah, so you are the French Ambassador! I am pleased to meet you. I have something I've been wanting to say to you."

Then he started talking at such a speed, stammering and making very little sense, that Countess H....., who was our interpreter, could barely keep up.

This left me the time to examine him properly. He had an abundance of long, brown hair, a bushy black beard, a high forehead, a large and prominent nose, and a forceful mouth, but everything about him drew one to his eyes, eyes that were pale blue and with an astounding brilliance and strange, compelling depth. His gaze was both sharp and caressing, innocent and astute, direct and distant. When his words took flight his pupils seemed charged with phosphorescence and magnetism.

This "man of God," this priapic mystic, was at least aware of his sins, because his whole presence, physical and spiritual, gave off a vile odor from quite a distance, a hot, bitter and bestial smell of the sort that you might expect from a billy goat.

In the course of the interview, which lasted almost an hour, I asked him frankly, "Is it true that you are trying to persuade the Empress to discontinue the war?"

He replied equally frankly. "Whoever told you that is an idiot. I insist on telling the Emperor that we must continue fighting until we achieve victory. But I also tell him that the war inflicts appalling suffering on the Russian people. I know villages where there is nothing left except widows, orphans, the blind and the maimed. It is unspeakable! For the next twenty years there will be nothing but suffering on Russian soil."

There you have it, and I have yet other proofs. This is how he talked about the war in front of the Emperor and the Empress. Such language contained nothing that would affront the Sovereigns, whose Christian souls made them profoundly sympathetic to the misery of the ordinary people. Indeed, it only served to touch their most tender sensibilities.

But then, in order to retain the favor of his august friends, this cunning fellow, having first moved them to pity, quickly consoled them with that bizarre, unexpected and illuminating eloquence that was his custom.

One winter day at Tsarskoe Selo, he discovered the Empress sobbing her eyes out. She showed him a dispatch from General Headquarters that had just announced the destruction of an entire army corps in a horrific massacre.

In response, while adopting a calm and sanctimonious authority, he said to her, "Do not distress yourself! When a *moujik* dies for his Tsar and his country, another lamp is lit before the throne of God!"

With such words, he moved the Empress to the bottom of her very soul.

Of necessity, I had arranged for Rasputin to be watched and informed upon, and I can assure you that I was kept fully up-to-date with his actions and his attitudes, but never did I hear that in any way he had persuaded the Emperor to start clandestine negotiations for a separate peace with the Germanic powers.

I therefore did not consider Rasputin to be an intentional German agent or any kind of spy who was acting as an intermediary or messenger for them, even though I believed him capable of any type of villainy.

First of all, he didn't need the money as he already received far more than he could use, given that he hardly spent any of it. He dressed like a *moujik*, and his wife and daughters dressed like paupers. He never ate at home. His pleasures not only did not cost him anything, they even made him richer. The women, young and old, who surrounded him were forever sending him food, clothing and gifts. The Emperor and Empress also heaped gifts on him. And the people who daily came to solicit his help also paid him liberally.

This saintly man therefore never lacked for resources; indeed he frittered them away without a second thought because he was very generous, especially toward churches.

But what made me believe above all that he was not in the clutches of the Germans was that he was totally incapable of playing any role, for the simple reason that he was utterly incapable of learning one. He was a primitive peasant, crude and ignorant. He was sly rather than intelligent, and had a short attention span. He did not understand a thing about politics. No one could have made him think or calculate in any way that was not already his custom. It was impossible to hold a lengthy conversation or serious discussion with him. He could only repeat the lesson that he had just been subjected to.

Having said that, I have no doubt that, via other intermediaries, the Germans were well served by him in the gathering of secrets relating to Russian strategy and diplomacy.

One of these intermediaries was Manus, the Jewish banker, whom I knew well. He put on a dinner for the *staretz* every week at which he could meet generals, the Emperor's aides-de-camp, top bureaucrats, and also several beautiful and accommodating women. The guests there would drink throughout the night, and warmed up by the wine, Rasputin would gossip and give his opinions tirelessly. All that he had learned from his conversations with the Sovereigns, all that he had confided in them or discovered of their opinions, their plans, their hopes and their concerns, he would spill out in lively tales ... And the next day, a full report would leave for Stockholm, where the German minister would send it on to Berlin.

Chapter 13

If you take a broad view of the history of the war and how it developed, you could say that, for France, the critical date was the month of September 1914 and the Battle of the Marne – the Miracle of the Marne. A smart observer could have said from that point that France would end victorious.

For Russia, the critical date of the war was the month of August 1915, when in Galicia, in Volhynia, in Poland, in Lithuania, and in the eastern part of Prussia – along the massive front that extended from the Baltic Sea to the Carpathians – the Russian armies, despite valiant feats of exceptional courage, could only retreat. At the same time, the internal disorganization of the Empire, the chaos in the administration, the economic woes, and the revolutionary fervor betrayed terrifying fault lines. It was already obvious that Russia could never fight its way to victory and that tsarism itself was in the greatest peril.

On September 3, 1915, I was obliged to send a telegram to my minister, M. Delcassé, warning him that the day was soon approaching when Russia would no longer be of any use to us as an ally.

> However uncertain this outcome may yet prove, nevertheless it must be taken into account in our governmental plans and in General Joffre's future strategy.

During these critical months of 1915, I had the opportunity to see the Sovereigns on several occasions and speak with them. I particular remember meeting them on June 19 at Grand Duke Constantin's funeral in the Fortress of Petrograd, where, in eloquent irony, the mausoleum lies right next to the state prison.

Nicholas II was wearing his campaign uniform and standing straight and still, so, as my place was just two paces away from his, I could study him at my leisure. Under the raw light that fell from the cupola, and the dazzling light of the candles that reflected off the icons, his face appeared thinner, his coloring whiter, and his expression mournful and distant, giving an overall impression of great sadness. To his left, the Empress, dressed in black, appeared radiant and attentive. Then, suddenly, her marble face blanched, and her breathing became arrhythmic and forced as her chest heaved. Somewhat against Orthodox customs, an armchair had been placed behind her because it was such torture for her to remain standing for long and the ceremony would last two hours. The poor woman was obliged to sit down four times, each time lifting her hand to her eyes as if excusing herself for her weakness.

On leaving the church, the Emperor signaled to me to join him for a chat and Alexandra Feodorovna joined in our conversation. We then proceeded to discuss only the bad news coming from the front that very morning. Everything they said suggested that both of them were resolved not to be defeated in the face of these misfortunes, but rather to reassert their commitment to building a renewed sense of national resistance by any means possible.

During this critical period, Alexandra Feodorovna seemed to re-experience, albeit much more intensely, the huge emotional shock that had seized her ten years earlier during the disastrous Manchurian campaign and the revolution that followed, frequently repeating to the Emperor, "You are the anointed of the Lord. It is from God Himself that you have received your sacred powers and it is to God Himself that you will have to account one day."

Nicholas II was in no doubt that his powers came from God and that he would have to account for himself one day in front of that same God. This was an article of faith with him, and an absolute belief. However, he all too often failed to make clear decisions when confronted directly with the daily problems of politics, while having continually to converse face-to-face with his ministers and to take into consideration the vicissitudes of public opinion and the declarations of the Duma. This was because he was a man of an indecisive and passive nature who was too easily influenced, even while being very suspicious.

He hesitated to make a decision, he put off meetings, he maneuvered, he evaded, he contradicted himself, and he gave in. In short, he lacked the gift that is indispensable for all autocrats – energy – and not just calm and persuasive energy, but also lofty energy, demanding energy, cutting energy, and, where necessary, the brute force and cruelty of Peter the Great, Nicholas I and Alexander II.

This energy, which is essential to an Autocrat's exercise of power, was possessed by the Empress and she was horrified that Nicholas lacked it. She was altogether a much tougher character than her husband, more strong-willed and determined, more high-spirited, more inclined to action, and with the more aggressive soul of a true sovereign.

Therefore, one could only approve of her actions when she exhorted the Emperor to appear more energetic, to behave more in line with the principles upon which the divine right of Russian Autocracy was based, and when, for example, she wrote to him at GHQ:

> *Stand firm, my love! Be masterful! That is what Russian needs from you. You have never failed to show your love for your people and your goodness. Now let them feel your fist. How many of them have said to me, "It is time to use the knout!" Everyone is demanding this. What a strange disposition is that of the Slav. When your love is not enough to drive the Russian people on, they must then learn to fear you.*

These impassioned exhortations were built upon a profound truth, that the Autocracy was not just the official form of government for Russia, it was also the basis upon which the rest of the structure of the country was fashioned. All of the everyday life of the people was integrated into the Autocracy, and without it they had nothing. Therefore, the destruction of the Autocracy would inevitably lead to the destruction of Russia.

Therefore for everything to work, the Autocracy needed to be led by an Autocrat. But since the war had broken out in its hurricane of violence, the Russian monarchy had offered up only the pitiful spectacle of an Autocracy deprived of its Autocrat.

In order to shore up her ideas, Alexandra Feodorovna turned to Rasputin for support and encouragement to refresh her ardor, and to tell her things like, "Oh that! But what does the Emperor think about this? Has he forgotten that God has put him in place to govern Russia? Why does he allow himself to be so influenced by his ministers? When he finds himself in the Valley of Josaphat, and has to render his account before God Himself, does he really think that the sclerosis and idiocy of his ministers will afford him any kind of excuse?"

And Rasputin didn't even hesitate to say such things in front of Nicholas II himself, who listened to him in confusion and fear.

One day, suddenly turning serious, he solemnly told the Sovereigns, "My life is a terrible test. I am persecuted as Christ was by the Pharisees. My enemies are determined to destroy me. May the will of God be done! But I warn you, should I die, you will lose your son and your crown within six months."

After that, the Emperor and the Empress were in no doubt that the future of Russia, and the safety of their son, rested exclusively in Rasputin's hands.

And the *staretz* soon found an excellent opportunity to manifest his omnipotence.

At the beginning of the war, Nicholas II had wanted to take supreme command of the armies, but all his ministers had counselled him against this move by arguing that he should not put his imperial reputation on the line by taking full responsibility for all military outcomes. Indeed, they said, it was essential for the running of the government that he should remain at the gates of the capital.

Bowing to these judicious arguments, he made Grand Duke Nicholas the Commander-in-Chief of the armies. Subsequently the Grand Duke went on to show exactly what he was made of and that, despite setbacks, he could inspire the devotion not only of his troops but of the whole of Russia in a commitment of blind faith.

Unfortunately, the Grand Duke had an implacable enemy in the person of General Sukhomlinov, the Minister for War, his rival for the role of supreme commander in July 1914. Since then, having failed to win this post, Sukhomlinov had ceaselessly exacted his vengeance on the Grand Duke. And, as he was sneaky, fiendish, devious, totally devoid of scruples, and surrounded by rogues, he prosecuted a terrible and insidious campaign against him, saying that the Grand Duke knew nothing of strategy and that he was incapable of drawing up plans, making decisions, or even seeing what was going on, so that he was forever being out-maneuvered by the enemy, and, as a result, his army had to pay for his ignorance and incompetence by being subjected to useless massacres.

It was easy for the Minister for War to spread these weighty accusations among the public, but he still needed an accomplice to help him undermine the Grand Duke in the eyes of the Emperor.

When Rasputin had arrived in St. Petersburg several years earlier, he had received a most sympathetic and warm welcome from the Grand Duke and his wife, Grand Duchess Anastasia, to the point where they had even attested before the Sovereigns to his supernatural powers, gaining for Rasputin their full confidence. But, little by little, the Grand Duke and Grand Duchess realized the extent of his contemptuous nature and repudiated him.

Several times, from the opening of the hostilities, the *moujik* had tried to renew his relationship with the Grand Duke, but in vain. The Grand Duke disdainfully kept his back turned toward him.

One day, Rasputin wrote to him that, "I am coming to see you at Stavka. Last night, the Virgin Mary appeared to me and told me that I must carry out a task for you," to which Grand Duke Nicholas replied, "I await your arrival, but I have to warn you that the Virgin Mary has appeared to me as well and has ordered me to hang you."

At the start of 1915, General Sukhomlinov assessed that the repeated defeats in Poland and Galicia, the incessant retreats of the Russian armies, and the general air of discouragement in the army offered him an excellent chance to reap his vengeance, so one of the freebooters by whom he was surrounded, Prince X....., took the matter to Rasputin, who took charge of the matter and approached the Emperor.

With thorough astuteness, the *staretz* did not only denounce the Grand Duke's strategic errors and his military incompetence; he forged from all quarters a much more damning and monstrous accusation: He claimed that the Grand Duke was at the heart of a sacrilegious conspiracy whose aim was nothing less than the overthrow of Nicholas II himself from the Russian throne, using the same summary proceedings as had previously ended the reigns of Peter III and Paul I. He did not provide the slightest proof of this plot; he merely limited himself to repeating the insidious whispering campaign that was already being conducted by the meretricious friends of General Sukhomlinov and certain venomous wastrels at court.

Given the Tsar's naturally suspicious nature, this accusation hit him full-on. Because he had been tricked so many times already, he didn't trust anyone, and he detected lies, subterfuge, treason and plotting wherever he looked.

For instance, did he not know that, in a cinema at the front he had honored with an imperial visit several days earlier, the audience had applauded the image of the Grand Duke like lunatics, while maintaining a disquieting silence whenever his image appeared on the screen? Did he not also know that, in certain salons in Petrograd where they willingly joked about the country's misfortunes, it was considered funny to invoke the spirits, in reference to nothing, of Tsars Peter III and Paul I?

Maybe he even knew about a grand duke, no less, who was known for his tendency for mockery and untrustworthiness, who amused himself one night in front of two ambassadors by propounding the following Machiavellian suggestion: "In a country where the government has absolute power, if the monarch becomes mad, he must be put down ... The necessary corrective for Autocracy is regicide ..."

Nonetheless, Nicholas II hesitated before makingchanges to the leadership of the armies during the most difficult phase of the war, at a time when the enemy's offensives were becoming ever more audacious and vicious. But the *staretz* was not short of arguments and switched the debate to an area where he knew in advance the Emperor would not dare to contradict him – matters mystical.

First of all he showed him that Grand Duke Nicholas could never succeed in any of his initiatives because he did not have God's blessing for them.

"Do you really think that God would bless the activities of a man who has betrayed me personally, the *Bojy tchelloviek*, the 'man of God'?"

Then, "You have no right to stay here in your palace when your country and your throne are in peril. At such a time, the Tsar's place is at the head of his armies. To cede his place to another is to offend God Himself!"

Then he came up with the ultimate argument, a theological one. "The Tsar is not just the temporal guide and leader of his subjects. The sacred unction bestows on him a much higher calling in this regard. He must be their representative, their intercessor and their protector in front of the Sovereign Judge. He must take upon himself all their worries, all their trials, and all their sufferings, to address them and give them weight in front of God."

Whereupon the Empress and Mme. Vyrubova would add their own moving appeals to supplement his eloquent exhortations, so that the Emperor ended up giving in.

One Sunday, on leaving Mass, he said to the Empress and Mme. Vyrubova, "Perhaps a sacrificial lamb is need to save Russia. I will be that lamb. May God's will be done!"

He called his ministers together the next day, and, in a curt tone, he gave them his decision as an act of his supreme will before which they must meekly submit.

Several days later, the Sovereigns arrived in Petrograd for the first time in such a long time that the sight of their retinue, and especially of their solemn bearing and grave expressions, summoned up an impression of doom wherever they went. They went first to the cathedral in the Fortress to pray before the imperial tombs. Then they proceeded to the house of Peter the Great to kiss the most saintly image of the Savior there, the one Peter the Great carried about with him everywhere. They then finished up their pious journey by visiting Our Lady of Kazan, where they spent a long time prostrating themselves before the miraculous icon of the Virgin.

On September 4, 1915, Nicholas II took full command of his armies at Stavka (GHQ), and that very night Alexandra Feodorovna wrote to him.

I cannot find the words to express what I feel; my heart overflows. I merely want to hold you in my arms and to whisper fervent words of love, encouragement and blessing. Oh how painful it was to let you leave by yourself, completely alone! But God stands right next to you, closer than ever.

With as much courage as determination, you are going to win a great victory for your country and for your crown. Never have I seen you so decided. You have shown your power; you have proved that you are an Autocrat, without which there will no longer be a Russia.

Therefore forgive me please, my angel, pardon me for having persecuted you for so long, but I knew your good and sweet nature! This time you needed to conquer yourself; you had to win the battle over yourself, alone against the world. God who is just, God who has placed you where you are, God who has anointed you to rule, He will protect you.

Also, day and night, the prayers of Our Friend will float up into the heavens for you and God will hear them. Grigory has told me this and I believe him absolutely. The glory of your reign now begins! Your sun will rise and shine out soon with a magnificent light! I repeat: God is with you and Our Friend is there for you as well!

Now, good night, my love; go and get some rest. May the angels bless you, my sun, the savior of Russia! Sleep well! But also remember last night when we were holding each other tenderly! I sigh for your caresses; I can never get enough of them.

I kiss you endlessly.

Your wife, Sunny.

After that, Nicholas II lived continuously at Stavka in Mogilev, 800 kilometers from Petrograd, and the Empress would remain alone in Tsarskoe Selo with their children.

On September 6, the Emperor, having taken full command of the armed forces and the navy, published the following order of the day:

With an absolute faith in Divine compassion, and an unbreakable faith in the final victory, we are fulfilling our sacred duty to defend to the utmost our country and we will not allow this land of Russia to be dishonored.

Beautiful words, but alas, although he pronounced them with absolute sincerity in his heart, he was no longer the one who was governing Russia. From now on, all imperial power was in the hands of Alexandra Feodorovna, who herself was completely dominated by, subjugated by and given over to Rasputin.

Besides, because she believed in him, how could she summon the force to resist him, and how could she be anything but delighted to obey with servility the man who said things such as, "Recently, God has again favored me with great revelations. I know that I will soon die amid atrocious suffering, but what can I do? Fate has given me the sublime mission to be set on fire in return for the safety of the Emperor, for your safety, and for the safety of the children and that of the whole of sacred Russia. Despite my appalling sins, I am a Christ in miniature, a little Christ of the sort you see in icons ... *Malenkii Christos*."

In front of the bedazzled and fascinated eyes of Alexandra Feodorovna, this despicable scoundrel became transfigured, haloed and rendered spirit as if by the light of Calvary.

Then, on the Thursday of Holy Week, April 20, 1916, when the Empress was receiving the Easter communion in the mysterious church of the court, the Feodorovsky Sobor, was it not astonishing that she asked Rasputin to receive the bread and the blood of the Savior at her side?

Chapter 14

Politically, the reign of the Empress and Rasputin would soon end up destroying the entire machinery of government. Not a single cog functioned properly, and everywhere there was disorder, incoherence and anarchy, not to mention the most appalling scandals because Rasputin was trailing behind him an unworldly clientele of braggarts and adventurers whom he had to satisfy.

In vain did Nicholas II try from time to time to stand up against the demands of the *staretz*, but if he delayed in giving his consent to Rasputin's wishes, the Empress would run to Stavka and not return to Tsarskoe Selo except in triumph.

Also during the year of 1916, all the ministers, even the most important ones – the Minister for War, the Minister for Public Works, the Minister of the Interior, the Finance Minister and the Foreign Minister – as well as the great administrative directors, the provincial governors and the chiefs of police, were continually replaced as if some kind of massacre had taken place. And these perpetual changes, which finally managed to ruin the reputation of the Tsar, took place in an atmosphere so capricious, so paradoxical, and so absurd that nobody knew whether to believe that the communications of the Emperor and Empress weren't trying to persuade them that black was white.

The reasons for determining whether a minister was in favor or disgraced went something like this: *He loves and respects our saintly friend … The fact that he loves our saintly friend so much is the result of God's evident grace.* Or, alternatively: *He spreads slanderous tales about our saintly friend … He smells of the Devil.*

The meetings of those co-conspirators, the Empress and the *moujik*, usually took place at Mme. Vyrubova's house and always in her presence. The best one can say about Mme. Vyrubova herself is that her rampant and roiling hysteria kept her in a garrulous and fevered state of agitation in which the silliness of her arguments remained imprisoned inside the confines of utter imbecility. There, in-between the orgies and the fornications, the *Bojy tchelloviek*, the "man of God," made his pronouncements in a mixture of menace, prophesy and ultimatums.

Just before the Emperor departed for Stavka, the *staretz* had given him several infinitely venerable icons representing the Divine Savior, the Virgin Mary, St. Seraphim of Sarov, St. Nicholas the Healer, St. George the Victorious, and so on, whereupon the Empress reminded the Emperor frequently that he must carry one of these images on him during all times of danger because their saintly friend had imbued them with an extraordinary efficacy.

But Rasputin went one better: he gave the Tsar a little tortoise-shell comb which he had subtly impregnated with his magnetic fluids, and the Empress yet again never failed to remind him that, before he made any important decisions, he must comb his beard and hair with it several times to clear his mind and strengthen his will.

She herself also received a precious talisman from Rasputin, an icon with a little bell that would ring whenever a person of evil intent approached her. Not only that, but for as long as she chose to keep this marvelous talisman, no enemy of the *staretz* would dare to ask for an audience with her.

By these means, Rasputin could get anything he wanted out of the Tsar, and here are some examples:

The previous March, General Sukhomlinov, the Minister of War, had lost his post because the number of scandals, crimes and prevarications associated with him had made it impossible for him to remain in office. Soon thereafter, the consequent public outcry had forced the Emperor to throw him in prison. However, it was just not acceptable to the *staretz* that one of his most notorious and devoted disciples should be treated in such an unseemly fashion.

But what was he to do, given that a military court had been set up and proceedings begun?

No matter! Rasputin demanded that the Emperor require that the court dossier be handed over to him so that he could expunge it, "otherwise there will be no way of saving poor Sukhomlinov."

Nicholas II did not give way immediately, judging that from a political and public relations perspective he must be seen to allow matters to take their course.

So the Empress wrote to him.

> *Our Friend insists that Sukhomlinov be freed,*
> *otherwise he will die in prison and things might*
> *turn bad. He adds, 'One should never hesitate*

to free a prisoner and to forgive a sinner who is on the road of righteousness. Prisoners are far more beloved of God than we are because of their great sufferings!'

Those were his exact words. Therefore, order at once that Sukhomlinov be set quietly free and place him under house arrest where he will be well looked after. I beg this of you, my love!

When the Emperor still appeared to hesitate to do as he was asked, the Empress sent him the following demand:

Telegraph the President of the Council immediately regarding General Sukhomlinov, and say this: "Having reviewed the dossier of enquiry in relation to the former Minister of War, General Sukhomlinov, I am of the opinion that the accusation is utterly baseless and therefore that the trial must be abandoned." This must be done immediately. I fear that I am being cruel in insisting that you do as I say, my sweet, patient angel, but all my faith lies in Our Friend, who only thinks of you, of our son, and of Russia.

Your little Sunny stands behind you like an immovable rock.

Endless kisses.

And the "sweet, patient angel", the feeble potentate, gave in to the immovable rock yet again.

Using the same devices, Rasputin forced on Nicholas II his own choice of Minister of the Interior, a man who had no other merits than humility and subservience – Protopopov. Rasputin went after this nomination with a particular asperity as it would bring with it enormous influence; the Minister of the Interior controlled the police, the military police, the Okhrana, and all the terrifying machinery of oppression and coercion associated with absolute power over an Empire of 170 million souls.

But Protopopov rattled Nicholas II's cautious nature. He was a man of around forty years old who, after erroneously spending a few years as a liberal, threw himself wholeheartedly into ultra-reactionary politics, taking up the causes of the "Black Bands," the silencing of the Duma, the censoring of the press, outright war against all forms of free thinking, a complete return to the most severe principles of conservative Orthodoxy, and as a prelude to all this, for his own amusement, a major massacre of the Jews.

Marching about and gesticulating wildly, with strange flames flashing across his eyes, he gave the impression of a man in a hallucinatory state, of a megalomaniac, and of a puppet.

He met Rasputin through the healer Badmaiev, the ingenious disciple of Tibetan sorcerers when he consulted this charlatan for a treatment of his awkward illness, an ancient malady whose symptoms in his case predicated a future of general paralysis.

And to add to his political talents, he had a remarkable gift for the occult sciences, especially for the highest and darkest of them all – necromancy.

The Empress embraced his cause immediately and tenaciously badgered the Tsar with, "He has been a friend of Our Friend for at least four years! Doesn't that mean that he can count on God's blessing?"

On October 1, 1916, Nicholas II appointed Protopopov Minister of the Interior, not realizing that by signing this order he was also signing his own death warrant.

In another sphere, Rasputin's blundering and tempestuous activities were even more disastrous, as he demanded that from now on he be consulted on military affairs, backed to the hilt, of course, by the Empress.

For example, she wrote to the Emperor:

> *Our Friend has been blessed this night with a celestial vision, in consequence of which he asks you to launch an immediate offensive against Riga …*

> *Our Friend is concerned that you have launched this current offensive without consulting him. It would have been better for you to have waited a while. Before knowing whether the time had come for an offensive, he immersed himself for*

a long time in prayer so that men would not be sacrificed in vain.

Our Friend sends his blessings to the whole Orthodox army and demands that you recall your great offensive in the North.

Tell me when you will start your offensive against Riga so that Our Friend can pray especially for its success. It is extremely important that you should do this ...

Reading these letters in which the gravest secrets of national defense were debated, where the life of Russia itself was in play, how can one not shudder when one knows with what kind of society of alcoholics, crooks, spies and bandits this "man of God" drank himself into a stupor every night?

Alexandra Feodorovona ill-health was a terrible trial to her during the closing months of 1916, as this regime, drenched in perpetual emotionality and ardent polemic, was exactly the opposite of what she needed to remain well. Her nerves deteriorated rapidly and the problems with her heart were incessant.

Nevertheless, a peculiar change could be detected in her character and her behavior. She was no longer, as previously, tired, inert, disabled, melancholic or taciturn – far from it. She was now hyper-active, loquacious, exuberant, irascible, impetuous and carried away. Now any new idea would grab her attention and dominate her spirit because she now believed herself designated by God to save the throne of the Romanovs and sacred Russia.

Already, earlier, the butcher's boy of Lyon, "M. Philippe," whose eyes penetrated deep into the unknowable world, had formally declared this mysterious designation, but the Empress had never dared to believe it, so, today, why would she not believe it with all her heart when Rasputin assured her of it?

Besides, hardly a day passed without her receiving letters and telegrams addressed to her by workers, peasants, priests, monks, invalids and soldiers. All these humble people, who were to her "the real voice of Russia," expressed their love for her, their gratitude, their devotion, the place she held in their prayers, the halo with which she was crowned and transfigured in their eyes.

For instance, they would write things like:

> Oh, our beloved Sovereign, mother and tutor of our adored Tsarevich …! Guardian of our traditions … Oh, our great and pious Tsarina … Protect us against those who would do us harm … Save us from our enemies … Save Russia!

Never did she suspect that these beautiful messages were in fact written within the confines of the Ministry of the Interior, who then had them sent from the provinces back to Tsarskoe Selo through the good offices of the police.

Finally, one evening, when receiving her new minister, Protopopov, did she not undergo the edifying surprise of seeing him abruptly throw himself to his knees in front of her and of hearing him cry out, his face in raptures, "Oh, Your Majesty, I see Christ standing right behind you!"

Meanwhile, along the immense front that stretched from the Gulf of Riga to the Danube (1,500 kilometers – the distance from Amsterdam to Toledo), the situation facing the Russian armies worsened every day. Having just joined the war, Romania had already lost 90% of its territories. And everywhere – in Podolia, in Volhynia, and in the Baltic provinces – the enemy continued its unstoppable advance. Would they not soon be in Kiev, Petrograd and Moscow?

From an economic point of view, the situation was just as alarming. The most critical products – bread, meat, kindling materials – were either exhausted or subject to a breakdown in distribution. Worse, this winter was going to be particularly harsh.

The major towns in particular were suffering from famine, while worry, irritation and discouragement were being talked about at the top of everyone's voices. The workers accused the ministers of deliberately starving the poor to provoke riots in order to have an excuse to crack down on Socialist organizations. In the factories, political tracts, originating in Germany or Switzerland, were secretly handed around announcing that the dawn of the revolution was nigh. In the barracks, the morale was so terrible that one regiment in

Petrograd, that had been called upon by the police to help maintain order, opened fire ... on the police.

A great howl of violent, bitter, wounded and exasperated recriminations rose up from every direction against tsarism, and as people always need to find a scapegoat, they concentrated their rage on the Tsarina.

The public had only a hazy awareness of the relationship between Alexandra Feodorovna and Rasputin. No newspaper dared attack the person of the Empress directly because the crime of lèse-majesté carried with it too high a price. However, the public was aware that the *staretz* had gained the confidence of the Sovereigns, that he could secretly enter the imperial palace, and that he now had an enormous influence over the government of the Empire.

However, whatever details were missing were richly supplied by the imagination, and when it comes to extravagance, there is no limit to the Russian imagination.

In Moscow in particular, the anger against the Empress burst its banks. People openly dared to denounce her in the streets, challenging her to come and show herself at the Kremlin and to risk making an appearance on Red Square, where she would be torn to pieces! They even went so far as to say that she could not remain on the throne and therefore needed to be sent to a convent at the first possible opportunity.

Everyone was talking passionately about a letter that Prince Lvov, the President of the Union of *Zemstvos*, had just delivered to the President of the Duma, describing in extreme terms the political peril facing the country.

The insane acts of those who govern us are destroying the fabric of the State. The perpetual coming and going of ministers is paralyzing the exercise of power ... But this is not all. A horrible suspicion, rumors of treason, and infamous reports have spread the belief that the hidden hand of the enemy is secretly intervening in public affairs.

This belief is seemingly confirmed by persistent references to the Government having already decided to negotiate a separate peace ...

The delegates of the Union of Zemstvos indignantly denounce the idea of securing a shameful peace! They believe that patriotism and honor dictate that Russia pursue the war all the way through to victory alongside our allies. They believe firmly in the triumph of our heroic army.

However, they are also obliged to recognize that the principal peril that faces us does not do so from abroad but from within our borders. They are therefore determined to support the Duma in its efforts to reestablish a Government capable of arranging for the availability of all the resources the country needs. Greater Russia will do whatever it can to help the Government of the people.

This eloquent message, filled with the fiery spirit of Moscow, aroused profound emotions in the corridors of the Duma, particularly among the more reactionary members who were the fiercest defenders of tsarism. And, indeed, the two leaders of the right, Count Vladimir Bobrinsky and Purishkevich, spoke for everyone when they courageously proposed to raise in a session of the Duma "the relations between Rasputin and the imperial court."

Therefore, addressing a silent, still and astonished assembly, they made a valiant charge to the last man against "the occult powers that dishonor and destroy our noble Russia," Purishkevich finishing by declaring, "I ask our ministers, if you are true patriots, to throw yourself at the feet of the Tsar and explain to him that the crisis that now faces us cannot continue, that the outrage of the people is building, that revolution threatens, and that an obscure *moujik* has no right to govern Russian any longer!"

During this campaign against her that was proving so damaging and threatening to her, Alexandra Feodorovna only saw the proof, the useless but inscrutable proof, that Providence was teaching her a great lesson.

"Yes," she told the Emperor, "I am well aware that many people detest me. I know that they even demand that you

124

send me to a convent. But that will not break me, that will not discourage me. I have from on high all the support I need and that no one can take away from me ... Even though I am ill and my poor heart is in such a bad state, I have more energy than all those who persecute me. I feel that I am more Russian than anyone and I will continue to work because I do it for you, for our son, and for sacred Russia."

And becoming wicked, implacable and "ferocious," she needled "her sweet, all-too-patient angel," to strike out without mercy at the enemies of the throne and of the country, reminding him of all the summary and bloody means of yore at his disposal, the only way he could discipline the anarchic instincts of the Russian people.

> Oh darling, remember that you are the supreme potentate! Crush your enemies! Be like Ivan the Terrible, like Peter the Great, like Paul I! No, don't laugh at me, you naughty child.

Nevertheless, however firm and brave she was in her convictions, she was also sad because Rasputin had become somber and sulky around her. Ever since the meeting of the Duma, he could only announce sinister portents that suddenly lit up the magnetic phosphorescence of his eyes.

"You will not see me much longer. As I have told you many times, I will suffer a terrible punishment that will destroy me, and the wind will disperse my ashes. Then you will lose your son and your crown. Then there will be a mighty uproar. Then Russia will fall into the Devil's claws."

125

One morning, on his way to pray at St. Isaac's with one of his mistresses, Mme. T....., he was walking along the dock on the Neva in a blizzard of snow. In front of the Winter Palace, he stopped for a moment, despite the storm, to contemplate the funereal décor of that great static and sad river, frozen as far as the eye could see in its coating of ice. Then, suddenly grabbing the young girl's arm, he cried out, "Oh, look at the Neva! Look at how she is red with blood!"

Not long afterward he became afraid of going out alone. He believed that he was being followed – tracked – in the street, so that he would continuously make sudden stops and look around him with haggard and furtive eyes as if he were a wild beast being hunted down.

At the same time, by a coincidence of fate, the Tsar and Tsarina heard of an unexpected death that seemed to confirm the threat of all the horrors to come as they had been predicted by Rasputin. This was the death of the French healer Papus the Magician, the hierophant and the man who had renewed interest in esoteric transcendentalism.

The Sovereigns met him in 1902, having been introduced to him by their great friend the pork butcher of Lyon, "M. Philippe."

Papus, whose real name was Dr. Encausse, used to come regularly to St. Petersburg and built for himself a large and fervent clientele there, because, from the time of Swedenburg and Baron Krüdener, all the spirits and all the enlightened ones, all the hypnotizers and the divines, and all the spinners of dreams and illusions received a sympathetic welcome along the banks of the Neva.

Early in October 1905, he was summoned to Tsarskoe Selo by the Sovereigns who had a pressing need for his insights during the terrible crisis that Russia was facing at that time. The disasters in Manchuria had aroused revolutionary forces in all parts of the Empire, along with bloody strikes, pillage, massacres and arson. The Tsar was in a cruel tumult, unable to decide between the conflicting points of view and urgings that his family, his ministers, his nobles, his generals, and all his court bombarded him with daily.

On one side, they claimed that he did not have the right to renounce his ancestral Autocracy and must press forward with all his force to crush the opposition; on the other side, he was urged to recognize the demands of the modern age and to introduce a constitutional monarchy into the country.

The exact day when Papus disembarked in St. Petersburg, a riot broke out in Moscow spreading terror because a mysterious trade union was calling out all the railway men on general strike. The magician was immediately summoned to Tsarskoe Selo, and after a quick consultation with the Emperor and the Empress, he organized a great ritual of incantation and necromancy for the next day.

Other than the Sovereigns, only one person – a young aide-de-camp – was present at this secret liturgy. Through an intense concentration of his will and thanks to a prodigious exaltation of his fluid dynamism, the "spiritual master" succeeded in summoning the ghost of the ever-pious Alexander III, with absolute proof that the invisible specter was indeed present, just as once, before the horrified eyes of King Saul, the Sorceress of Endor had summoned the shade of Samuel, who predicted King Saul's defeat at Gelboa, followed by an appalling death.

Despite the anxiety that was plucking at his heart strings, Nicholas II calmly asked his father whether he should confront the current of liberalism that threatened to drag Russia under. The ghost, "the indestructible spirit of the bones," the Zelem of Nephesh, replied, "You must crush this embryonic revolution at any cost. But it will arise again one day and will prove to be as violent as today's repression will have been at its worst. No matter! Take heart, my son! Don't give up!"

While the astonished Sovereigns mulled over this shocking prediction, Papus assured them that his magic powers could conjure away the predicted catastrophe, but only while he remained on "this physical plane." Then he solemnly carried out a series of rites to protect them.

Now, since October 26, Papus the Magician no longer occupied this "physical plane," and all the forces he had been conjuring up to protect them had been destroyed.

So the revolution was coming!

On December 25, the Tsarina traveled to Novgorod the Great, accompanied by Mme. Vyrubova, to carry out certain specific devotions she had set her heart on.

Under a pale and snow-laden sky, the ancient and proud city of the Rurikovich family, whose motto of "You don't fight against God or Novgorod the Great" forcefully expresses all the disenchantment that is left behind after a great dream has been fulfilled.

After a lengthy mass at the Cathedral of Saint Sophia in front of the icon of the Virgin Mary that "cries when Novgorod endures too much suffering," Alexandra Feodorovna was taken to the Monastery of the Dime where the relics of St. Barbara are carefully guarded.

But what particularly attracted her about this convent was that she wanted to see a very old nun who was already considered to be almost a saint, "the truly humble sinner" Marie Mikhailovna.

Since time immemorial, this nun, who claimed to be one hundred and seven years old, had been enclosed in a dark and narrow cell wearing heavy chains that mortified her body, and despite the fact that she could no longer remember having washed, she emitted no odor.

Under the protection of a supernatural grace, all the acts of penitence of the body and the mind that overwhelmed her provided her with a sweet and constant joy, a gentle smile, and a spirit of extraordinary insight.

Sometimes even, however much a stranger she was to the most notable realities of the exterior world, she had marvelous intuitions and a prophetic understanding of the present and of the future.

And when the Empress entered her darkened cell, simply lit by a candle, she was greeted with the words, "I see that the Empress and Martyr Alexandra Feodorovna approaches me."

Chapter 15

On December 30, Grigory Efimovich Rasputin was murdered by Felix Yusupov, a young dilettante who immersed himself in wayward tastes and perverse fantasies, and who was a great admirer and emulator of Oscar Wilde.

Fearing he might lose his nerve, he had recruited an additional four accomplices.

Prepared well in advance with Machiavellian sadism, the crime was carried out at night with such a shamefully laid trap, and employing such treachery and cowardice, that the disgrace of the assassins matched that of their victim.

On hearing the news, Alexandra Feodorovna initially lost her mind, overcome by a fit of dizziness as if an abyss had opened up before her. Then she sent a telegram to the Emperor at Stavka begging him to return to her immediately.

Her upset was exacerbated by the unbearable anxiety caused by the deep mystery that surrounded the event.

She knew on the evening of December 29 that the *staretz* had disappeared from his lodgings, but that is all she knew. The murderers had planned the whole thing so skilfully that the *moujik's* body couldn't be found. Even the mighty Okhrana, that magnificent instrument of investigation and coercion, the Tsar's Pretorian Guard, that had immediately rallied all its forces as if Russia was facing a national emergency, couldn't dig up any more than vague hints and contradictory information.

The newspapers were silenced by the censor, so the public believed all the rumors that came their way – and the wilder they were, the more they were believed – rejoicing that this "dirty dog" had been killed and rushing off to Our Lady of Kazan to light candles. The women in particular became fascinated by the mysterious tragedy, and while they were standing in line at the bakers or butchers to receive their meager daily rations, they told each other that Rasputin had been killed during an orgy, swearing that every little detail they had just invented was true.

Soon, via reciprocal auto-suggestion, they had pieced together the horrendous truth, such that "Grand Duchess Tatiana, the Tsar's second daughter, was a party to the crime in her disguise as a lieutenant of the Horse Guards, because she wanted to take her revenge on Rasputin who had tried to rape her one night in her bedroom. She had therefore watched on as his body was lacerated with blows and she had even been there to see him castrated before her very eyes!"

This nonsense soon spread everywhere and was believed as an article of faith.

In the end it was mere luck that set the Okhrana on the right path because Rasputin's body was discovered deep in the River Neva, near Krestovsky Island, covered in such thick ice that there was an initial reluctance to identify him formally.

His body was taken in secret to the Chesma Military Hospital which lay between Petrograd and Tsarskoe Selo. After his autopsy had been carried out, his remains were left in the care of a nun at the Okhtay Convent called Sister Akulina, whom Rasputin had known while he was alive because he had once exorcised her under strange circumstances. By order of the Empress, only she and a nurse were allowed to prepare his body; nobody else was allowed near him, not even his wife and his daughters, and his most devoted followers begged in vain to be permitted to see him for the last time.

The pious and once demonically possessed Akulina spent three hours washing his body, embalming his cavities, dressing him up in new clothes, and placing him in his coffin. Then, as a final gesture, she placed a crucifix on his chest and a letter from the Empress in his hands.

My beloved martyr, bless me so that your benediction will follow me constantly as I pass along the road of sorrow for as long as I remain on this earth. Remember us from upon high in your prayers!

Alexandra

The coffin was driven to Tsarskoe Selo around midnight to be interred in a chapel that was in the course of being constructed in the grounds of the imperial park. The only people present were the Emperor, the Empress, the four Grand Duchesses, Minister of the Interior Protopopov, Mme. Vyrubova and the officiating priest of the court, Father Vassiliev.

Now that her friend was lying in the sacred ground of her church and that she could go each day to pray at his tomb, Alexandra Feodorovna became calmer, and gradually her sorrow gave way to reasoned acceptance and complete submission to God's will.

For Nicholas II, the initial shock had been no less brutal because he immediately remembered Rasputin's terrifying prediction of, "If I die, you will lose your son and your crown within six months."

On January 7, 1917, a week after the assassination of Rasputin, I had the opportunity of an audience with the Emperor because I needed to communicate to him my opinions on the more pressing diplomatic and military questions of the day. The audience lasted two hours and it was certainly the most intimate conversation we had ever had together.

I left him filled with sadness and anxiety. His words, and especially his long silences, his tense bearing, his distracted and distant air, his sudden losses of concentration, and all his vague and enigmatic nature confirmed for me a suspicion I had been harboring for several months, that he was overwhelmed by events, that he no longer had any faith in his mission or in his work, that he had so-to-speak abdicated in his mind, and that he was resigned to a future of catastrophe and sacrifice.

Chapter 16

The death of Rasputin served as a tolling of the bell for tsarism, and within several days – indeed within several hours – the whole panoply of Russia began to collapse in on itself.

On March 12, 1917, revolution broke out and on March 15 the Emperor abdicated.

On March 21, the entire imperial family – or as they would be known from now on, "the Romanov Family" – were placed under arrest in their palace at Tsarskoe Selo in the name of the people.

At the beginning of the crisis, while the garrison of Petrograd rebelled and the popular hurricane unleashed itself, while the feeble Duma trembled in the face of the violence, and while the sudden collapse of governmental authority led to fire and blood in the capital, Nicholas II still retained supreme command of his armies at his General HQ at Mogilev. Alexandra Feodorovna was therefore alone at Tsarskoe Selo with her children.

Initially she did not understand the grave implications of the events that were taking place around her, or rather she refused to do so. Then she saw with her own eyes all the beautiful Imperial Guards regiments, the magnificent Cossacks of the Escort and the court police throwing themselves eagerly into the arms of the triumphal revolutionaries. And she saw even worse still: she saw that she was being abandoned by her closest servants, and by those who most owed their high offices, titles, epaulettes, braids, decorations, ornamentation, privileges, and all their histories of ostentatious and fabulous favor to the Sovereigns.

And to make a bad situation worse, her son and her daughters were succumbing to a dangerous case of the measles – with complications that included pustules and pneumonia – so that while the palace was in complete disarray, the poor woman had to nurse them day and night.

But the very worst aspect of her torture – or of what she called her "nightmare" – was that she was kept in complete ignorance of what had happened to the Emperor, although she knew that his generals had abandoned him, and feared that, after having the cowardice to seize him "like a mouse in a mousetrap," they might have forced him to lay down all his powers as Tsar and Autocrat so as to concede a liberal constitution to his people.

This idea "killed" her because, in abdicating the sacred powers he had been accorded by Divine Providence, he would be committing the most irreparable error imaginable and damn himself in the eyes of God.

Finally, after a week of this nightmare, she saw her husband arriving back at Tsarskoe Selo as a captive, his body so emaciated that it was as if he had suffered a long illness. Quickly he said a few words to reassure her. No, he hadn't betrayed the sacred law he had solemnly sworn to uphold on the altars at the Kremlin; he had stepped down from the throne but he hadn't signed a full abdication of tsarism. The inviolable principles of tsarism and the Orthodoxy remained unviolated.

But if he had the right to remain at peace with the religious aspects of his conscience, he had equally wished to carry out to the very end his weighty duties as the Commander-in-Chief of the Russian armies.

On March 21, he published a message of farewell to his armies that was his testament as a sovereign, or better still his testament as a patriot, and whose generous notes should have a place in the historic record:

> *For the last time, I address you, my much-beloved soldiers!*
>
> *Since I renounced, in my name and in the name of my son, the throne of Russia, all power has been transmitted to the provisional government which has been formed by the imperial Duma.*
>
> *May God grant His aid to this government in conducting Russia toward glory and prosperity! May God grant His aid to you as well, valiant soldiers, in defending your country against a cruel enemy!*
>
> *For more than two and a half years you have suffered at every hour a punishing test of service; much blood has been spilled, enormous efforts have been accomplished, and already*

the hour approaches when Russia and its glorious allies will crush with common intent the supreme resistance of the enemy.

This unparalleled war must be carried through to absolute victory. Whoever contemplates peace at this time is a traitor to Russia.

I have the firm conviction that the boundless love that fires you up in the name of our beautiful country has not been extinguished from your hearts. May God bless you and may St. George, the great martyr, lead you to victory!

Amid the sudden crumbling of all their sovereign power that had covered them as a reflection of divine majesty, the Sovereigns were further struck in the most sensitive point of their being by an inhuman profanity that filled them with shock and horror.

On March 22, around nine o'clock at night, the coffin of their saintly friend Rasputin was secretly exhumed from its chapel at Tsarskoe Selo where it was resting and taken to the Pargolovo Forest fifteen versts north of Petrograd. There, in the middle of a clearing, several soldiers, commanded by an ingenious officer, dug up a large tree trunk. Then, having forced open the coffin, they removed the body with sticks, because they didn't want to touch his putrid body, and lifted it, not without difficulty, onto the trunk. Having sprayed the body with petrol, they proceeded to set fire to it, the cremation lasting the six hours until dawn.

Despite the glacial wind, the length and complexity of the operation, and the billows of acrid and pestilential smoke that arose from the brazier, several hundred *moujiks* crowded all night around the fire, silent, unmoving, and contemplating with a fearful stupefaction the sacrilegious holocaust slowly devouring the martyred *staretz*, the friend of the Sovereigns, the *Bojy tchelloviek*, the "man of God."

When the flames had finished their work, the soldiers collected up the ashes and buried them under the snow.

The instigators of this sinister epilog had precursors in the Italian middle ages. The human imagination does not indefinitely find new ways to express its passions and its dreams.

In the year of grace 1266, Manfred, the bastard son of Emperor Frederick II – who was the usurper King of the Two Sicilies, an assassin, a perjurer, a seller of favors, and a heretic, whose reputation had been sullied by every crime that one can imagine and who had been excommunicated by the Church – perished at the hands of Charles of Anjou as they fought on the banks of the River Calore, near Beneventano.

His captains and his soldiers, who adored him because he was young, handsome, generous and charming, gave him a touching funeral on the exact spot where he had died. But, a year later, Pope Clement IV proscribed against this scoundrel, who was unfit to lie in sacred ground, the papal procedure of anathema and malediction. On his orders, therefore, the

Archbishop of Cosenza exhumed the corpse and fulminated over Manfred's unrecognizable remains the damning sentences that would send his excommunicated soul to hell: *"In ignem aeturnum judicamus"* [We condemn you to the eternal fire].

This office was carried out at night by torchlight, the torches being extinguished in turn until everything was left in complete darkness. After this, Manfred's remains were scattered across a field.

This tragic and picturesque scene violently stoked the emotions of contemporaries and inspired Dante to write one of the most beautiful passages of his 'Divine Comedy.'

The fires of Pargalovo also lit up the final image of the Siberian *moujik* in a Dante-esque glow. But, among all those condemned to the circles of hell, among all the *"perduta gente"* [lost souls] whose crimes had condemned them "to eternal misery," are there many people who could challenge Rasputin for his energetic behavior, for his vigor, for the audaciousness of his magnetism, or for the intensity of his demonic expression?

Chapter 17

In the month of August, the sickly Provisional Government, overwhelmed by the tide of revolution and trembling with fear in the face of threats from the Bolshevik Soviets, realized that the imperial family could no longer stay so close to Petrograd where their lives were now at risk. They therefore decided to transfer them to Tobolsk, the first stage on the great Siberian road, a very calm little town that was hard to reach by rail and whose inhabitants still remembered them fondly.

Nevertheless, for the prisoners, leaving Tsarskoe Selo for Tobolsk, which they reached on August 26, this represented a most painful ordeal. While the house they had been allotted was comfortable enough, it was surrounded by a wooden wall and guarded like a prison.

The Provisional Government allowed the ex-Sovereigns to choose which companions they wished to take with them into their captivity. Several of the people on whom they had heaped much honor – for example, Naryshkin, their most intimate and greatly favored aide-de-camp – proved to be of such low character as to abandon them. However, in contrast, they found that their general aide-de-camp Tatiscchev, the Marshal of the Court Prince Dolgoruky, their Maid of Honor Miss Hendrikov, their reader and companion Miss Schneider, Dr. Botkin, and the Tsarevich's tutor Pierre Gilliard remained proudly loyal to them. M. Gilliard's loyalty was particularly to be commended as his Swiss nationality might have been considered to have absolved him from all further responsibility toward them.

Closed off from the world and subjected to a rigorous regime in which their every movement was spied upon, the prisoners lived an extremely monotonous, restricted and difficult life, and the incessant liberties their guards took with them would have been enough in themselves to make their situation almost unbearable.

They particularly resented being deprived of news about political events, but they certainly heard in November that the Petrograd Soviets had overthrown the Provisional Government and that Lenin had taken all power into his own hands. And, as Christmas approached, they learned of the appalling progress of the Boshevik dictatorship, of the terror that had been unleashed against the whole of Russia, of the consternation and massacres taking place in the heart of the system of government, of the pillaging and destruction of the churches, and of the desecration of the most respected sanctuaries and relics.

Truly, Rasputin's prediction was coming true to the letter, "When I die, Russia will fall into the Devil's claws."

Nicholas II felt a bitter sadness as he heard this news. This is what his abdication had amounted to! In renouncing his throne, he had believed that his personal sacrifice would rapidly dispel the hatred that had built up against his regime, and that the Russian people would quickly become reinvigorated and have no other thought than to fight against its national enemies, as in 1812. Now he knew the magnitude of his error.

Soon he would learn that the dictators in the Kremlin were to surrender to the Germanic forces by signing the unspeakable Brest-Litovsk Treaty, thereby condemning Russia to suicide and dismemberment. Just a few lines written by them were sufficient to destroy all the political work of the great Orthodox tsars whom history had justly termed "the gatherers of the Russian lands." And, when all the newspapers also referred to a clause under which the Germans would have demanded that the imperial family be delivered to them safe and sound, the Emperor cried out, "If this is not a trick to dishonor me in the eyes of my people, no one could have performed a worse outrage against me."

The Empress also protested in her astonishment, saying, "Owing our safety to the Germans? Never! It would be better to die at the hands of the Bolsheviks!"

On top of the pain of their memories of their former private life and their humiliation in front of the Russian people, the imperial family had to undergo material hardships which became stricter and more severe by the day. The small garrison of Tobolsk that was originally intended to guard them was replaced by members of the Red Guards who were unkempt, arrogant and needling, and who were particularly inconsiderate in front of the young Grand Duchesses. Despite implementing strict economies, the money finally ran out and some servants had to be dismissed because they were down to "soldiers' rations."

These tensions in her reclusive life drove Alexandra Feodorovna ever deeper into her mystical attachments. The image of the Savior constantly shone out before her eyes, and every time she was insulted by a member of the Red Guards, she calmly declared, "Let us not fight against this as it is God Himself who is sending us this humiliation. Accept it for the sake of our eternal souls. Before dying on Golgotha, did Jesus Christ not empty the chalice down to the last drop?"

On March 20, as Easter approached, she wrote:

> *The Savior of the world is coming! Let us bow before his cross; let us courageously help him carry it; let us always remember that our own crosses are barely a shadow of his cross ... When they abuse you and insult you, be patient! When they torment and persecute you, rejoice!*

She wrote this prayer for one of her daughters:

> *Oh Lord, give us the patience to withstand, in these stormy days, the cruelties of our torturers! Help us to suffer through the shame and insults visited upon us! At the gates of the tomb, give us the superhuman force to pray humbly for our enemies!*

She also wrote this prayer:

> *Queen of Heaven and Earth, she who consoles the afflicted, hear our prayers! I beg you to look*

down upon our country. Sacred Russia, our luminous home is on the point of dying. She must not be abandoned! I beg you to look down upon our tears and our martyrdom!

Chapter 18

On April 22, Basil Yakoblev, a delegate of the Central Committee, arrived in Tobolsk from Moscow with extraordinary powers that allowed him to shoot anyone, immediately and without trial, who disobeyed his orders. On his arrival, he told "Nicholas Romanov" that he had been sent to take him, his family and his retinue "on a journey to a secret destination that would last four or five days."

When pressed by the Emperor as to why this should be and where they would be going, Yakoblev was evasive in his responses. But several bizarre words that escaped him persuaded Nicholas II that the Bolshevik dictators were determined to return him to Moscow because they had promised the Germans that he would ratify the Brest-Litovsk Treaty.

This assumption made him cry out, "Me? Me? You expect me to sign the Brest-Litovsk Treaty? I would rather cut off my hand!"

He left at three o'clock in the morning of April 26 in the company of the Empress and their daughter Marie. Everyone else would follow on later.

"Nicholas Romanov and his dependents" were given a very simple and strongly barricaded house to live in – the "Ipatiev House." Superstitious as the Sovereigns were, the name of "Ipatiev" must have made some impression upon them because it was at the famous monastery of Ipatiev at Kostroma in 1613 that the founder of the Romanov dynasty,

Michael Romanov, received envoys from Moscow offering him the throne as Tsar Autocrat. Would two events be presided over by a kind of fate – the glorious beginnings and the tragic end of a dynasty?

The Sovereigns immediately realized that from now on they would be treated with neither respect nor mercy.

First of all, five of their companions and most of their servants were led away, to be sent far from Ekaterinburg or to be imprisoned in the local town jail.

Then, the position of commanders in charge of the Ipatiev House were given to two Jewish commissars, Jacob Yurovsky and Chaia Goloshkin, both of them crazed Bolsheviks whom the Central Executive Committee in Moscow had furnished with secret orders and unlimited powers.

In order to keep the prisoners more securely under guard, Yurovsky installed himself in a bedroom on the second floor of the Ipatiev House from which he could keep an eye on everything that happened in this narrow imperial lodging. Additionally, he placed guards in all the corridors and in front of all the doors.

This regime was therefore even worse than in Tobolsk and rendered the prisoners' lives so intolerable that this prayer of the Empress could be understood only too well:

> Queen of Heaven and Earth, do not turn away your eyes from our martyrdom! Oh Lord, You who see us at the gates of the tomb, give us the superhuman force to pray humbly for our torturers!

Around July 12, Yurovsky and Goloshkin became particularly and visibly agitated because much was happening in the Urals. For several weeks an army of counter-revolutionaries — the "White Army" commanded by Admiral Koltshak and supported by two divisions of Czechs who had previously been prisoners of war — was making its approach from Eastern Siberia, relentlessly pushing back the Red Army as it went so that it appeared that nothing could stop it entering Ekaterinburg.

In the face of this threat, Goloshkin hastened to Moscow to receive his final orders from Lenin as to what should be the fate of the Romanov family.

The evening of July 16 passed as usual for the prisoners. After a very simple supper at eight o'clock, they tried to entertain each other somewhat by playing cards. Then, shortly afterward, gripped again by somber thoughts, they returned to their favorite pastime, reading aloud several chapters of the Gospel and then several passages from the Prophets.

At 10:30, they went to their beds because the ailing Empress was tired.

However, three hours later, the clumping of heavy boots in the next room awakened them suddenly. The door opened. It was Yurovsky with an escort of guards.

In his unhinged voice, he commanded them, "Get up and get dressed quickly! We are going to take you somewhere else because the White Army is approaching Ekaterinburg."

As soon as they were ready, they were taken to the ground floor into an empty, low, dark room. All the prisoners of the Ipatiev House, all eleven of them, were assembled there: The Emperor, the Empress, the Tsarevich, the four Grand Duchesses, Dr. Botkin and three domestic servants.

A Red Guard said to them, "Wait here! Some cars will come to collect you in a few moments."

However, it would appear that the prisoners had no idea of the danger they were in, and, when they had been waiting some time, the Emperor asked for chairs to be provided for the Empress and the Tsarevich as they couldn't stand much longer.

Chairs were brought, but a second later the door burst open and the Bolshevik Commissar entered with a revolver in his hand, followed by about a dozen soldiers. Without a word, Yurovksy signaled to the soldiers to fire on Nicholas II who was taken by surprise as he fell. Then came a terrifying noise and a hail of bullets, and all the other prisoners slid to the floor amid a sea of blood. The whole episode only lasted two minutes.

But the murderers had not yet completed their work. They had only carried out the easiest and least repugnant part of their task. What remained was much more disconcerting, sinister and ignominious, because now they had to make the eleven bodies disappear without trace in accordance with their instructions from Moscow. Everything that had just taken place was being controlled down to the finest details by the Central Executive Committee of the Kremlin, by Lenin, Trotsky, Sverdlov, Zinoviev and Djerzinsky. The Ekaterinburg Soviet can claim no greater role in the historical record than as those who carried it out, as bearing only the modest glory of having been the executioners.

Through heightened precaution and to avoid any defiance of orders by Russian soldiers at the critical moment, the dictators of Moscow ordered that several Germans should be slipped into the firing squad. One of these Germans, who was evidently cultured but disdainful of his historic notoriety (as he did not sign his name), succumbed to a moment of poetic intent on the eve of the massacre while receiving his final instructions from Yurovsky in the execution chamber.

Picking up a pencil, he amused himself by scribbling on the wall two verses by Heinrich Heine, who must have been turning in his grave.

Beltazar ward aber seltiger Nacht
Von seinen Knechten umgebracht
15 VII 1918

[But Belshazzar, that very night
By his own men was killed outright]

What remained now was to make the eleven bodies disappear so that they would never be found again.

Under the watchful eyes of Yurovsky, the murderers quickly loaded the dead bodies, still warm and bleeding, into a truck, then, at great speed, they headed for a forest that stretches out for some distance from Ekaterinburg – the Koptiaki Forest.

After several long detours along tracks that were hard to navigate, they stopped at a clearing in the center of which there was a shaft leading down into an abandoned mine, a spot that had been carefully scouted several days area.

There, keeping watch, they proceeded to empty the truck, but not before stripping the victims' bodies of prized items: pious and beloved mementoes that had never left them, medallions, bracelets, rings, icons and pendants. Then they stripped the bodies of their clothes, turning them over and manhandling them. Then, using large butchers' knives, they dismembered them and cut them into pieces, pouring ninety kilograms of sulfuric acid over the remains in order to dissolve the skin and bones. Then, they poured two hundred liters of petrol over them and set them on fire. Finally, after completing this entire set of nauseating operations, they shoveled the stinking residue, the combined slops that were left behind but had no substance in reality – described by Bossuet as, "a don't know what that has no name in any language" – down into the mine.

This is how it all played out on the world stage on July 16-17, 1918, in one of the most hideous scenarios ever devised by the great playwright of mankind's evil intent.

Conclusion

This long martyrdom that was so heroically endured without a single protest born of resistance or fear, without a whisper of complaint or a groan of self-pity, represented the true human and Christian crown worn by Tsarina Alexandra Feodorovna, the only crown that could strengthen her reputation, excuse her and absolve her before the court of posterity.

There is no doubt that heavy charges still weigh against her memory, and there is no doubt that, despite excellent intentions, and despite her most noble and courageous soul, Alexandra Feodorovna spelled disaster for her country, her husband, her children, and not least for herself. All her acts seemed cursed, reminding us of the most star-crossed heroines of Greek tragedy.

But the verdict of historians would be too unkind to her if they stopped there.

One of the techniques Rasputin used most often to break down her self-respect and dominate her entirely was to say, "When you find yourself in the Valley of Josaphat, you will no longer wear an imperial crown on your head. You will appear before God in the full nakedness of your soul. And that day, you will no longer be proud ..."

Turning these words of the *staretz* into profanities is of little use as they dictate our conclusion.

While we try to forget the political role of Alexander Feodorovna, and while we try to depict her no longer wearing an imperial crown on her head but in her intimate conscience – "in the full nakedness of her soul" – one single sentiment fills us and blots out any other – that we should feel pity, an immense pity, for her.

End